The Greatest Miracle

The Greatest Miracle

Unveiling God's Greatest Gift to You

Donald Ogolo

WESTBOW
PRESS
A DIVISION OF THOMAS NELSON

ISBN: 978-1-4497-2085-8 (sc)
Library of Congress Control Number: 2011932967

WestBow Press books may be ordered through booksellers or by contacting:

WestBow Press
A Division of Thomas Nelson
1663 Liberty Drive
Bloomington, IN 47403
www.westbowpress.com
1-(866) 928-1240

Printed in the United States of America
WestBow Press rev. date: 7/18/2011

Some Bible Quotations have been paraphrased to enhance clarity.
KJV- King James Version (1769)
WNT- Weymouth New Testament Translation (1912)
WEB- Webster Bible (1883)
GWV- God's Word to the Nations Translation
YLT- Young's Literal Translation (1898)
CLV- Concordant Literal Version
EMTV- English Majority Text Version
MLB- Modern Language Bible

"To the Holy Spirit, my own "Paddy" partner and Senior
Consultant in this family business, for His inspiration"

AND

"To everyone that feels a sense of fear, guilt, uncertainty and
solitude within, and in need of the salvation, deliverance
and healing power which only Jesus can provide"

"For whoever calls on the name of the Lord shall be saved"
(Romans 10:13)

Contents

Introduction

...in heaven, something very significant was about to happen. A high-powered meeting of the trinity- God the Father, Jesus Christ, and the Holy Spirit was taking place. They all sat on a round table and laying bare before them was the earth in complete chaos, void and formless. The agenda was set, the discussions began, plans were unraveled and these three beings got set to implement their plan.

The Holy Spirit stepped down on to the earth and roamed through out this chaotic place, inspecting it as a professional Engineer would do before constructing a road. God the Father then spoke the Word, Jesus Christ was the channel and the Holy Spirit transformed the Word into its equivalent concrete form. He gave life and meaning to the spoken word. The trinity then inspected all its creation and found it to be perfect. What a wonderful architect in the Holy Spirit!

Not yet done, on the sixth day of recreation, another very important round table meeting took place in heaven. The trinity met to finalise plans on the creation of something very special and greater than all the creations. The plan was carefully executed. God created this special something and His Holy Spirit happily obliged to reside in it, and it instantly came to life just as every other touch of the Holy Spirit in creation gave life. God then at a special ceremony proudly unveiled this special thing before everyone in heaven. The angels marveled and shouted for joy. Heaven celebrated and this special thing was given authority over all the earth while God ruled heaven. But what was this very special thing that so excited the trinity and threw heaven into great celebrations? That thing is YOU! God specially creates every human being on earth and is overjoyed by his or her creation. You are very special indeed!

I have good news for you- salvation is not far from you!

"The word is near you, in your mouth and in your heart...that if you confess with your mouth the Lordship of Jesus and believe in your heart that God has

raised Him from the dead, you will be saved…for whoever calls on the name of the Lord shall be saved."

- Romans 10: 8, 9, 13.

Even if you were the ONLY ONE on earth, Jesus would still have died for you!

Chapter 1

In the Beginning...

$\mathcal{T}$he creation of you, me and every other human being on this earth was never a coincidence. Our creation was carefully and wonderfully planned out by trinity- God the Father, God the Son (Jesus Christ), and God the Holy Spirit. It utmostly excited the heart of trinity at our creation.

The Creator's Masterpiece

After God had spent five days recreating the lands, sea and air animals and plants, He decided to create something much more special. He decided to create someone more like Himself who would rule the earth while He ruled heaven. He decided to create a superior creature, one He would constantly fellowship and have a wonderful time with. To do this, the Divine Council of Trinity met in heaven and on a round table sat God the Father, God the Son, and God the Holy Spirit. The plan to create that special thing called man was placed on the agenda. Just as the royal palace of Trinity was heaven, that for this special creature called man would be in the place called earth. Since it is not worthy of a king to rule in a empty and chaotic palace, God had spent the previous five days furnishing and organizing this palace called earth for man to have absolute authority over. This really excited the God Head. It was agreed that man was to have dominion on earth while they ruled heaven, and that man was to be in every way like them. On the sixth day of recreation, the plan was fulfilled. God created the spirit of man, in His own image, and formed a body out of the dust of the earth for it. More wonderfully, He breathed into man the Spirit of life and man became a living being. [Gen. 2:7] There was a roaring applause in heaven as man was created. The Trinity was extremely ecstatic and expectant; the angels danced and rejoiced at this glorious creation of man. Man was the highest of all the creation and God really loved him. God subsequently gave him dominion over all the earth. This creation was in the Garden of Eden. God walked with this man (called Adam) closely as he went through the garden to exercise this dominion given to him and his race by conferring names to each creature God had created. God wore large smiles as He heard the names given by Adam to each creature. They were the very best of friends and God was very fond of Adam.

Faithfulness of a Friend Put To Test

The loyalty of man was put to the test when God instructed him to be at liberty eating of any tree in the garden but not to eat of the tree of the knowledge of good and evil which was in the midst of the garden. He was also informed of the consequences of disobedience to this command- death (see Genesis 2: 9, 16, 17). God made woman, a helper for Adam. Adam gave her the name Eve. Adam failed this test when he ate of the tree of the knowledge of good and evil after his wife gave him a fruit of this tree. The consequence of this was both spiritual and physical death. Spiritual death because the wonderful relationship between God and man was broken and man now saw God as an enemy. Physical death because the life of man on earth was surely to reach an end after he lived a certain time on earth. Man had sinned and incurred the curses and penalty that came with sin. Sin simply means acting contrary to the command or word of God. With this sin by Adam came in sickness, struggles, pain, frustrations, sorrows, toiling and death. The curses and consequence of this sin by Adam was passed on to his future generations and that meant every human being born into this world. Adam had sinned for everyone and so death came to his entire race, Rom. 5: 12, 19 for by the law of God, the soul that sins shall die. Ezek. 18: 4

The one behind the scene

Sin took its origin from the devil, the greatest enemy of man. It was the devil that enticed man to make an attempt at the fruit of the tree of knowledge of good and evil, and Eve in turn passed it on to Adam. The devil used the serpent as his instrument in enticing Eve. Gen. 3 The devil as we know him today was known as Lucifer and was of the order of a Cherub, one of the highest orders of angels in heaven that minister unto

God. Isai. 14: 12- 17; Ezek. 28: 11- 19 Lucifer gave sin its definition when he attempted to exalt himself above God who created him. He won over a substantial number of angels to himself, and led a rebellion against God with the purpose of overthrowing Him. He was however defeated and thrown down from heaven and the dominion God had given him on earth as a cherub was taken away from him. Knowing well that God hated sin, he offered man a taste of sin and created an enmity between God and man. The human race that lived before the race of Adam (pre- adamite race) gave themselves to these sins and this caused God to destroy the earth of that time by a deluge. Jer. 4: 23- 26 After a while God decided to recreate the earth with living creatures and this new creation was that of Adam. This is where Genesis 1: 2 commences. The waters of Genesis 1: 2 was the result of the deluge that destroyed the pre adamite race.

In the new Adamite race, the devil also went to work. He likewise introduced sin to Adam and Eve and by this an enmity was created between God and man. But God had already made a provision for man's redemption even before he sinned. Rev. 13: 8 By this sin, man gave the devil the dominion that God had bestowed on him and so man was left without authority and power on earth. This is likened to a military officer who plans a *coup* against a government, successfully overthrows the government and takes the authority and power of that government. Before man fell, the order of power and authority in descending order was- Trinity, then man, then godly angels, then the devil and his angels. When man sinned and gave his authority to the devil, the order then became- Trinity, then godly angels, then the devil and his angels, and then man. Man was now at the bottom of the ladder and how pathetic it became. He made the devil the god of this world (1 Cor. 4: 4). Jesus Christ however came and restored man to a far higher position- as joint heirs with Him to the throne. This privilege is reserved only for those that receive Him into their lives (that is, become born again). And so, every sinner is at the bottom of the ladder and is trampled upon at will by the devil and his agents. Jesus, when he came down from heaven and took the form of man, Php. 2: 7- 8 was Himself made lower than the angels. Heb. 2: 7

God makes a way

Man by sinning against God had brought condemnation upon himself. He was sentenced to death. God who is love itself 1 Jhn. 4: 16 is also a Holy and Just God. A holy God demands payment for sin; a Just God cannot "sweep sin under the carpet." If not, God would not be Holy and Just. The only way out for man was for a perfect sacrifice to be offered, for

"Without bloodshed there is no forgiveness of sins" [Heb. 9: 22]

The sacrifice had to be spotless; that is, without sin. However, man could never pay for his sins and still live because the payment for sin required death. Moreover in the first instance no man was spotless because every man had sinned and fell short of God's glory. [Rom. 3: 23] So where would that perfect sacrifice come from? Who could save man from the death penalty and curses that hung on his neck? To further complicate issues, instead of looking for ways to redeem himself and appease God whom they had offended, man kept on heaping up sins before God (see Isaiah 43: 22-24). They invented new methods of committing sin. Anyone would have expected God who is too holy even to behold sin [Hab. 1: 13] to have instantly wiped out the human race as He did in the time before Adam and in that of Noah, but His deep love for man was unsurpassing. Even the angels in heaven ponder over what could make God still love these tiny creatures called humans even when they rebel constantly against Him. Since man was helpless regarding his fate, God decided to step in and rescue the same humans that continually rebelled against Him.

Another meeting of the Divine Council of Trinity was called in heaven. At the meeting was God the Father, God the Son (Jesus Christ), and God the Holy Spirit. The main agenda for the meeting was the salvation of man and his restoration to a perfect relationship with God as it was when they were first created. Jesus Christ agreed to leave His majesty and equality with God the Father and God the Holy Spirit and come down to earth, adopt the lowly form of humans, and offer Himself as that perfect sacrifice which humans could not provide. He agreed to carry upon Himself the entire sins of man and its consequences so man could be free from them. He agreed to take upon Himself all of man's murders, sexual immoralities, idolatry, abortion, lies, revelries and all their consequences-sickness, poverty in all dimensions (physical, spiritual, moral), frustrations, sorrows, struggles, such like there, and ultimately death. It was to be a payment by substitution at a costly price- He was to shed His spotless blood by being brutally scourged and humiliated in a most cruel way by death on a cross. By that, the death sentence and curse that brought pain, sickness, frustrations and such like there would be taken away. The only role man was to play to partake of the privilege was to receive His offer of salvation by faith. After Jesus Christ (God the Son) had finished His work of redemption on earth, He was to be taken up, back into heaven, and glorified, and God the Holy Spirit would then come down to earth and live in everyone that received the salvation of God the Son and be a seal on them as citizens of heaven, and continue the work from where Jesus left off through such believers. The deal was sealed and execution of the plan was fixed for a certain time ahead.

When the set time for revelation of this salvation arrived, Jesus Christ gloriously stepped down from heaven on to the earth to be born of a woman and of the Holy Spirit. Heaven was in a jubilant mood with ceaseless and indescribable celebrations. In fact, jubilant angels came down to earth, visited shepherds and joyfully announced the good news to them. [Luk. 2: 8- 15] In complete disparity, the earth was quiet, not knowing what great event had happened. The salvation from God which He had long hinted through the Prophets was finally revealed to the earth. Jesus Christ later on fulfilled the prophecies by dying on a cross for the salvation of man. By His death, Jesus had offered that spotless sacrifice which man could not give. He had paid the price for man's salvation and freedom by His own blood. The curse was also taken away. Only those that received Him into their lives, just as Trinity had ratified in heaven before unveiling the salvation to the earth, enjoyed this new privilege. And so, those that do not receive Him are still under the penalty of death and under the curse.

Jesus Christ by His work on the cross, took man up the ladder of authority and power – to His level; a level far above the devil and his angels. The authority of man which he had given to the devil was restored by Jesus Christ. The devil and his agents were so soundly defeated on the cross that Jesus made a public spectacle of them, [Col. 2: 15] as was the custom in the ancient Roman Empire in which an opponent when defeated was openly displayed before crowds. After He resurrected, His work on earth was done. He carried His very own blood and ascended into heaven, then went right to the throne of God and presented His blood which He had shed for the complete salvation of every human being. With that, He took the highest position of authority by sitting at the right hand of God the Father. Every power in the universe- in heaven itself, on earth, in the sea, and beneath the earth- was placed under Him, that at His Name every knee (power) should bow and every tongue should confess that He is Lord. [Php. 2: 9- 11] On taking His rightful place at the right hand of God the Father, it was now time for the Holy Spirit to mount on to the stage fully; this time in the disciples. He had been promised to the disciples by Jesus, [Jhn. 14: 15- 18; 16: 7, 13] but would come only after Jesus was glorified. Now that

Jesus was glorified, it was time for the Holy Spirit to "run the show" in and through the disciples for the glory of Jesus. Jesus on getting to heaven and presenting His blood to the Father secured the release of the awesome Holy Spirit on to the earth to live within those that received Him as Lord and Saviour. It was the presence of the Holy Spirit that brought the life which Jesus had to the Christian, and which sealed the Christian believer as a true candidate for heaven. The Holy Spirit was also to convict sinners in the world of their sins and lead them to salvation in Jesus Christ, through the believers. On the day of Pentecost, forty-nine days after the resurrection of Jesus, the Holy Spirit who had been much promised stepped down gloriously from heaven on to the earth and lived in everyone that had received Jesus Christ as Lord and Saviour. This same Holy Spirit has been with us on this earth ever since and has not gone back to heaven, as He usually did intermittently in the Old Testament period. This is the result of the blood of Jesus which cleanses the believer and makes him a purified home for the Holy Spirit to abide permanently, rather than intermittently as previously in the Old Testament period. He still carries out the same works as He did in the period of the Apostles of Jesus and dwells (Grk. "*oikeo*" meaning "to make a home" with the idea of being relaxed and feeling comfortable in a home) in everyone that receives Jesus Christ today. It is His dwelling in an individual that gives that person a citizenship status in heaven; otherwise there is no hope of heaven for such a person.

Saved by Good Works?

No man is ever saved by good works, in spite of how good those works might be. Man is saved ONLY by believing in Jesus Christ. You must know that man did not become a sinner by committing sins on this earth. He rather became a sinner because of the sinful nature transferred to him by Adam, and only Jesus can take away that sinful nature. This is why notwithstanding how charitable, loving, caring, philanthropic a person might be, if he does not receive Jesus into his life and get saved, he is headed for torment in hell. The intrinsic sinful nature that was transmitted to him from Adam instinctively condemns him to hell.

Take an example, in the region of Caesarea was a man called Cornelius. Acts 10: 1- 48 I do not think there was any as self righteous as Cornelius in that region. Scripture described him as a devout man, God fearing, very generous and charitable, and very prayerful too v. 2 Now what else would anyone need? But wait a minute! This same Cornelius was bound for hell because he was not saved by the blood of Jesus. Despite his fantastic religious *résumé*, the sinful nature transferred to him from Adam had already condemned him to hell and unless he was born again, he would perish. So devoted was he to God that this caught the attention of God who had to send His angel to him. He and his entire household not only got saved by the instrumentation of the Apostle Peter, but they also received the wonderful baptism in the Holy Spirit. God truly loved Cornelius as He does every human being He has created. Receiving the message of salvation is a wonderful privilege anyone can have. It is a great demonstration of love on the part of God.

We are not saved by works of righteousness which we have done but by the mercy of God...whom He poured out on us abundantly through Jesus our Saviour; ^{Titus 3: 5, 6} for our righteousness are like filthy rags before God. ^{Isai. 64: 6} God acknowledges only the righteousness of Jesus which is given to believers when they receive Him. ^{2 Cor. 5: 21} For as by one man's (Adam) disobedience many were made sinners, so also by one man's (Jesus) obedience many will be made righteous. ^{Rom. 5: 19} God never hesitated in giving out His BELOVED and ONLY BEGOTTEN Son Jesus to save people who had wronged Him, to save sinners; and Jesus Himself never cared so much about His glory, splendour and majesty but thought of the helpless and pitiable state of man and offered His life as a sacrifice for their salvation and freedom, even when the converse should have been the case.

Why do men still love to die?

Why do men still love hell? Why do they still prefer death even when God has made a way out for them? A very alarming question indeed. The act of God in saving man was never in anyway cheap. It cost God His dear Son Jesus and it cost Jesus His life. Yet God still offers this salvation to man as a free gift, but man still throws the gift back at the face of God as if saying, "Thank you Sir, but I don't need it. You should not have wasted your time making that sacrifice. It was not necessary anyway." Rejecting Jesus is like spitting at the face of God and trampling upon Jesus' blood before God. Let no one ever think it was an ordinary thing God did in sending His Son Jesus into the world to save sinners. Scripture says

"For God SO LOVED the world that He gave His only begotten Son..."
Jhn. 3: 16

7

Donald Ogolo

Whenever God referred to Jesus in scripture, He did not just call Him "My Son" but 'My BELOVED Son." That showed how dear Jesus was to Him, yet He never thought twice about sending Him down to earth to save man. Those that love hell truly do not understand the significance of the work of Jesus on the cross. The angels of heaven must think at times what manner of creature man is. Just a little smile from God towards them would make their entire day. One can then only imagine what they would do if God would go as far as giving His Son Jesus to die for them. They realize and understand the importance of the good gestures of God. Many of them certainly wish they were in the place of man to cherish the wonderful privileges given to man. They would be envious of man if it were left to them. By far contrast, many on earth regard the privileges of God as inconsequential even when the angels in heaven yearn to have it. Men still love to die. Men still love hell. Hell holds no good for anyone. The devil, the enemy of Jesus and man, has been condemned to the Lake of fire and he would certainly feel lonely there with his angels. Accordingly, he strives to lug in men with him to hell. Roads lead from earth to hell but NO road lead from hell to earth, and so once a visitor in hell always a host in hell.

Chapter 2

What it Means to be Born Again

When God created man, He created him spirit, soul and body, in that order. The body or flesh was the least in significance while the spirit was the highest. The spirit is what gives you a consciousness of God. The soul gives you a consciousness of YOURSELF. The body acts as a house for the soul and spirit. God interacts with you directly through your spirit and not your soul or body. This is because God Himself is spirit John 4: 24 and this is why He created man a spirit, in His own image. Read what Job says in the book of Job 10: 8- 12:

"Your hands have MADE me and FASHIONED me, an intricate unity; yet You would destroy me.

Remember, I pray, that You have MADE me like clay. And will you turn me to dust again?

Did You not pour me out like milk, and curdle me like cheese,

Clothe me with skin and flesh, and knit me together with bones and sinews?

You have granted me life and favour, and Your care has preserved MY SPIRIT."

Job had the knowledge that he was a spirit being, and he regarded his skin, flesh, bones and ligaments as the clothes (outer coverings) of his spirit man.

The soul is the seat of your emotions, will and intellect and this is why it gives you self consciousness. It is what makes you distinct from

9

other human beings. The difference between man as God created him and the lower animals is that while man has a spirit (Greek "*pnema*"), the lower animals do not have a spirit but rather have a soul (Greek "*psuche*"). In other words, while man as he was originally created had "God- consciousness", the lower animals do not have this, but have only "self- consciousness". The body on its part is NON LIVING, in the sense that it only acts as a casing for the spirit and soul. It is what keeps your spirit and soul right here on earth and makes other human beings visible to you. It is under the direct influence of the spirit or the soul. In other words, every visible action of yours in actual fact is not being done by the body but by your spirit or soul. The body is what gives you world consciousness. *God CREATED man a spirit, in His own image, and MADE a body for him. The body was made to enable this spirit man exist and function on earth, and interact with other earthly creatures and materials. The Hebrew word used in Scripture for create is "bara" literally meaning to form something out of nothing. The Hebrew word used in Scripture for "made" is "asah" meaning to form or mould something out of an existing thing. Only God has power to create. Man only makes out of his discovery of what God has already created. It is remarkable to know that the word "created" is used 45 times in 38 verses in Scripture and the word "create" is used 8 times in 6 verses, and in all these instances, they are associated ONLY with God.*

With the order of spirit, soul and body in place, God had a wonderful time of fellowship with man in the Garden of Eden. Man had complete consciousness of God and the network between God and man was unhindered. However when the loyalty of man was tested in the garden using the tree of the knowledge of good and evil, God clearly laid out the consequence of disobedience,

*"For **in the day** that you eat of it you shall SURELY DIE"* Gen. 2:17

The death referred to here was a spiritual death. Death means a separation from life. So, man would be separated from God spiritually if he disobeyed, the same God who was the source of his life. Adam, the first man, went on and disobeyed God, and upon him and by extension his descendants was poured the penalty of spiritual death. With the spirit now dead, the order was reversed to body, soul and spirit. Man now became more soulish (self conscious) than spiritual (God conscious) and all his life tended towards this trend. This trend was then passed on to his generations. So every human being born is naturally soulish; very self conscious. The death of the spirit brought an interrupted fellowship with

God because God never interacts with the soul or body. They are in fact His enemies. [Rom. 8:7]

As would obviously follow, all the benevolence of God was also hindered and this brought about sickness, affliction, sorrow, struggles, frustrations, and such like there. The enmity between God and the flesh (body) is unsurpassed. Sin thrives when the flesh is in control. Genesis chapter 6 describes the very pathetic state to which man had fallen and how God felt about it. The flesh had so much taken control of man that sin had now become mere triviality. And here is how God reacted to the situation. First, God had thought that His Spirit could in some way convict man of his sinful ways and cause him to repent. But the Spirit of God so struggled and struggled with man's heart, to direct him back to God, the source of his life. After much struggle, man refused to yield himself to God's loving Spirit, and God's Spirit gave up. Why did man refuse to yield to God's Spirit? God Himself tells us why in verse 3:

"...for he is indeed FLESH"

The flesh had taken so much dominion over man that there was no leeway for the Spirit. Despite all efforts by God to restore the broken fellowship with man, man was unyielding because the flesh was in control. Only a loving God could go this far. Secondly, the direct consequence of the control of the flesh was that the wickedness of man became GREAT in the earth [v. 5] and the directions of the thoughts of his heart were ONLY EVIL CONTINUALLY. [v. 5] This was a very pitiable situation and it showed the despicable level to which man had attained. How did God feel about it? First, "He was sorry that He had made man on the earth" [v. 6]. Only sin could make a God who is love itself [1 John 4:8] feel this way! Second, "He was grieved in His heart". "To grieve" used here means "to cause EXTREME and INDESCRIBABLE pain or sorrow". It similar to losing a loved one to physical death. It conveys the same meaning as grieving the Holy Spirit. [Eph. 4: 30] God's heart was broken and if He could cry, He certainly did! His beloved creation had turned their backs on Him and gone astray. The consequence of this fleshly control was the destruction of that entire generation except Noah and his family. [Gen. 7: 17- 24]

This trend of body, soul and spirit had continued down the generations to this present generation, and with this trend, the enmity between God and man continued just as it was when Adam fell through sin. Every human being, once born into the world acquires this trend. This is the first birth of any human being. This is birth by human flesh, and as such he that is born in this way is flesh. ^{John 3:6} Flesh can only give birth to flesh just as a dog can only give birth to a dog. More importantly, flesh cannot inherit the kingdom of God ^{1 Cor. 15: 50} or receive eternal life. Now what must you do to receive eternal life? The answer is simple- you MUST be born again.

It is called "born AGAIN" or "born FROM ABOVE" (heaven) or "born ANEW" because your initial birth into this world was your first birth and was through the instrumentation of humans (your parents) which are flesh. Now being born again, you are miraculously born the second time, this time not by any human instrumentation but by water (the word of God) and by the Spirit of God. ^{John 3:5} It is NOT a reformation of your old nature, but a creative act of the Holy Spirit. Now since you are not this time born of the earth, but from above (heaven), you are now a citizen of heaven. This is the ONLY criteria to partake in the kingdom of God. This only happens when you accept Jesus Christ into your life as your Lord and Saviour. The Spirit of God then comes into you and abides with you, and by Him your spirit man comes alive again ("resurrected from death"), and the fellowship between you and God is restored. That becomes your "spiritual birthday". A very significant truth about being born again is that Jesus Christ by His Spirit now living in you imparts eternal life to you. You are saved from eternal death. You become a child of God, because as many that receive Jesus Christ, He gives the authority to become children of God. These are those who are not born of the flesh or of any man, but who are born of God. ^{John 1:12, 13}

A certain Pharisee (a lawyer) by name of Nicodemus came to Jesus at night^{John 3:1- 21} and the purpose of his visit was based on the signs (miracles) which Jesus had performed among the people ^{John 3: 2} but Jesus emphasized the greater importance of being born again over miracles. One can be healed of any sickness but still end up in hell. One can be raised from the dead but still end up in hell. One may be delivered of an affliction but still end up in hell. But no one can be born again and end up in hell! Little wonder, it is His greatest gift to man and He emphasized it in His ministry while here on earth. When you are born again, the Spirit of God abides in you and the blessings of God find a home in your life.

WHY YOU MUST BE BORN AGAIN

Do not be surprised that you must be born again, for he that is not born of God cannot see the kingdom of God. ^{John 3:3} Whoever is not born again is no different from the lower animals which have self consciousness but no God consciousness. Once you receive that new life imparted to you by the Holy Spirit through Jesus Christ, your body becomes dead because of sin but your spirit comes alive because of righteousness; not your righteousness but that of Jesus Christ which He has imparted to you. ^{Romans 8:10} With the spirit which was once dead now alive, God through His Spirit now controls you. If you are led (controlled) by the Holy Spirit, you are a child (an heir) of God. ^{Rom. 8:14} By this, there is no condemnation whatsoever hanging over your neck for you are no longer led by the flesh but by the Spirit. ^{Rom. 8:1}

What being born again DOES NOT mean

- Belonging to a church- One is not born again by this or even regularly attending church services. Not everyone attending church services belong to the TRUE church. The true church is the body of Jesus Christ, ^{Eph. 4: 12; 5: 23- 32; 1 Cor. 12: 27} and whosoever does not belong to Jesus (that is, believe in and receive Him) is not part of His church but is rather only deceiving himself.

- Philanthropy- Again, giving to the poor and needy or even making donations to any institution including the church itself, does not make you born again and saved; even if you give out all your wealth to the church of God. No man can buy himself into heaven. The only way to heaven is Jesus. No amount of money or possessions can measure up to the soul of any man. Nothing on earth or in heaven can buy or redeem the soul of any man except the blood of Jesus.

- Being born to parents who are serving the Lord Jesus in any capacity does not make you born again. Even if your entire ancestors from both your maternal and paternal lines were archbishops or General overseers of churches, that does not grant you a place in heaven. Aaron, the high priest of Israel during the time of Moses had served God very faithfully, but when his sons Nadab and Abihu sinned against God by offering strange fire unto Him, they were instantly destroyed. Not even Aaron's position as high priest of Israel could stop the Holy God from pouring out His wrath upon the disobedient sons. Lev. 10: 1- 7

- Being extremely religious- observing regular fasting and prayer, paying tithes, not indulging in sexual immorality, revelries, lies, drunkenness, and such like there does not make you born again. Cornelius observed these Acts 10 but was still on his way to hell.

The list is endless. But the summary of it all is this- whoever has not accepted Jesus Christ into his life as Lord and Saviour is NOT born again, irrespective of who they are or what they do or the associations they have.

Chapter 3

Sickle Cell Genotype Turned Normal by Faith in Healing Covenant

"*In that day the deaf shall hear the words of the book, and the eyes of the blind shall see out of obscurity and out of darkness*" (Isai. 29: 18)

Healing and the New Covenant of Salvation

Our God is still in the healing business and always will be as long as we live on earth. He is the Lord, the eternal, self-existing One, and He does not change. ^{Mal. 3: 6} He is the same yesterday, today, and forever. ^{Heb. 13: 8} Salvation is a covenant between God and the believer. Now briefly, there are certain elements of every covenant made between God and man:

1. The superior being usually initiates the covenant. Examples can be seen in those between God and Noah; ^{Gen. 6: 18; 9: 9} God and Abraham. ^{Gen. 17: 1- 16} In all these, God initiated the covenant, being the superior one. Notice that God referred to the covenants made with man as *"My covenant"*, and not "the covenant" or "your covenant". Reference is usually made to the covenants as being God's covenants.

2. There were always two parties involved- God and man, or God and a nation, or God and a family.

3. There MUST be a mediator or a sacrifice (bloodshed) between the two parties involved for the covenant to become effective. In other words, a life must be laid down at the altar of sacrifice

before the covenant takes effect. The blood that is shed ratifies the covenant and makes it legal (lawful and recognized) and binding before God. Infact the Hebrew word used in scripture for covenant is *"beriyth"*. It means *"to cut through"*. It was derived from the fact that the animals used for the covenant had to be cut in two pieces, with the contracting parties passing between the divided parts of the animals. And of course, when divided, the blood of these animals were spilled. The whole idea behind this was that the party that first contravened the covenant was to be cut in two like the sacrifice. The corresponding Greek rendering in the New Testament is *"diatheke"*, bearing a similar meaning to the Hebrew rendering. The need of blood for ratification of the covenant is because before God, the life of every creature is in its blood. [Lev. 17: 11] Blood can be comparable to an ink used to sign bilateral agreements between peoples and nations, without which there will be no evidence of an existing agreement between the parties involved.

4. The offspring of the other party partaking of the covenant benefited from the blessings and promises of the covenant.

5. Every covenant between God and man, whether conditional or unconditional, came with promises and blessings from God. For conditional covenants, man had to keep his own part in the terms of the covenant.

6. There was a term or witness to the covenant.

7. There was an effect to this covenant, such as change of name or building of an altar.

8. In a conditional covenant, there were penalties for flouting it, just as the Hebrew translation of the word "covenant" suggests. Just as the descendants benefited from the blessings of the covenant, so did they sometimes suffer when it was flouted.

9. Each covenant brought in a new dispensation in the dealings of God with the human race.

In all, there are eight covenants in scriptures made by God with man:

1. **Edenic covenant (Gen. 1: 26- 28; 2: 15- 17).** God made this covenant with the newly created man (Adam) in the Garden of Eden. It was a covenant of fruitfulness and dominion. The penalty for contravention was death. This covenant ushered in the dispensation of innocence.

2. **Adamic covenant (Gen. 3: 14- 17).** This covenant was a direct consequence of the failure of man in the first covenant. It entailed a newly conditioned life of hardship and sorrow for man- for Adam, through the curse on the earth; and for his woman, through childbirth and subjection to the man. [v. 16, 17] The death penalty was enforced and the serpent by which the devil enticed and deceived man was also conditioned to a new kind of life. [v. 14] The devil was as well sentenced to a complete and permanent defeat by the seed of the woman. [v. 15] This covenant extended to the descendants of man, and through it came the dispensation of conscience.

3. **Noahic covenant (Gen. 8: 20- 22; 9: 1- 17).** God made this covenant with Noah after He destroyed the earth by a deluge in His wrath. This covenant was one of fruitfulness for man and beast on the earth, and for the continual existence of the earth. The sign of this covenant was the rainbow. This covenant steered in the dispensation of human government, with the enforcement of capital punishment for murderers.

4. **Abrahamic covenant (Gen. 12: 1- 3; 15: 18; 26: 24, 25).** This was made with Abraham, after God chose and called him out of the entire human race to fulfill His plans for humanity through his descendants. It was one of blessings for Abraham and his descendants, through whom the Messiah (Jesus Christ) was to come. This ushered in the dispensation of the promise. The sign of this covenant was the circumcision of every male child born to his family. It lasted until the giving of the law in the time of Moses, a period of about 427 years.

5. **Mosaic covenant (Exod. 20 to 24: 1- 8).** It is also called the Old Covenant or Testament, a name from which the first part of the bible (the Old Testament) is derived. This covenant followed the giving of the Law to Moses and the children of Israel. This thus ushered in the dispensation of the law. The Law consisted of three parts:

❖ The commandments (Exod. 20: 1- 26) - which expressed the will of God for the children of Israel.

❖ The civil laws (judgments) (Exod. 21: 1- 23: 33) - which regulated their social life.

❖ The ordinances (Exod. 24: 12- 31: 18) - which regulated their religious life.

This covenant was ratified by the sprinkling of blood upon the book of this law and upon the people. ^{Exod. 24: 1- 11} This covenant was conditional, demanding death to anyone that transgressed it, even if it was only one of the commandments, ordinances or civil laws. It likewise brought life to the one that kept every bit of it, not faltering in one of it.

6. **The Land covenant (Lev. 26; Deut. 27:1- 30: 20).** This covenant is also called the Palestinian covenant. This was made with the children of Israel and states the terms by which they should possess and continually abide in the land of promise. The Lord gave a promise to Abraham that his descendants would completely inherit the land of Canaan (Palestine), but here God gives the people conditions by which this will be fulfilled. They did inherit the land, but never completely, and they were occasionally exiled from the land because they flouted the terms of this covenant by sin against God.

7. **Davidic covenant (2 Sam. 7: 1- 17).** This was made with David and his descendants, and the blessings consisted of securing of the house, throne, and kingdom of David forever, and a sure place for the people of Israel forever. It is an eternal covenant. Disobedience to God resulted in punishment, but not annulment of this covenant.

8. **The New Covenant (Heb. 8: 8; Matt. 26: 28; 2 Cor. 3: 6- 18).** It is also called the New Testament, from which the second part of scriptures is derived. It includes all the blessings and promises found in the New Testament of scriptures. This covenant is the eighth between God and man in scriptures. Eight spiritually signifies a new beginning, and every other covenant made between God and man in scriptures was a pointer in some way to this New Covenant. This New Covenant is between God and believers, and is a covenant of salvation. ^{Jhn. 3: 16} The mediator of this covenant is Jesus Christ. The

blood He shed (Heb. "*shaphak*" and Grk. "*ekcheo*" meaning to "gush out" or "spill forth" like a spring from the ground or a volcano from its source) on the cross is the sacrifice. His blood was His life that was shed for the remission of sins. It was necessary for it to be spilled forth if this covenant was to be effected. You partake of this new covenant by surrendering your entire life to Jesus- by believing in Him and in His finished work on the cross. This is your own role in the terms of the covenant. The role of God is to grant you this salvation and bring you into the promises and blessings which He has entrenched in this covenant. Like the other covenants, there are blessings and promises for everyone that partakes of this new covenant of salvation. These blessings include deliverance, protection, Gift and gifts of the Holy Spirit, healing, and much more. Infact, ALL blessings and promises in the New Testament belongs to the believer. Even if healing is just one of the numerous blessings and promises in this covenant, healing is sometimes referred to as a covenant because of its viewed prominence relative to other blessings. It is infact part of the New Covenant. And so, many people hammer so much on healing that they forget that God has given them greater and many more blessings when they come under this covenant through salvation.

If you partake of this covenant, you are entitled to these blessings and promises. You do not beg for them, but they are yours by right. **The partaker of any covenant with God is BY RIGHT entitled to ALL the promises and blessings that God outlines in the terms of the covenant.** This is how a believer should approach scriptural blessings. You just receive them by faith because you are now a partaker of the covenant with God and they are yours by right!

The same cannot be said of unbelievers (sinners) or those who are either out of the covenant (backsliders) or who have breached a term in the covenant (for example, a believer living in sin). In these situations, God is by right not obliged to keep His own part of the bargain. He could however, by His mercy and for His own purpose, bless someone in any of these categories, but such people cannot be one hundred percent sure of receiving from Him. For instance, God could heal a sinner out of mercy and for His own purpose of using that act to bring the sinner and other unbelievers to salvation in Christ Jesus. Notwithstanding that, the sinner can never lay claim or right to healing or deliverance as can the believer. If God refuses to bless them, He cannot be blamed for it. God works on principles, and not sentiments. True, over ninety-five percent of the miracles Jesus performed while on earth were on sinners, but this was in the old covenant; the new covenant had not yet been ratified because His blood had not yet been shed. More so, this was for the purpose of bringing them to repentance and salvation.

The blessings and promises of God in the new covenant are all established in the salvation of Christ Jesus, and those outside it cannot lay claim to it. Today, you see unbelievers lay claim to promises in scripture and speak them into their lives in the believe that it would take effect; but this is only a waste of effort. You can hear some proclaim:

"I shall lend to many nations, but I shall not borrow. The Lord will make me the head and not the tail; I shall be above only, and not beneath…" (Ref. Deut. 28: 12, 13); or

"I will decree a thing and it will be established for me…" (Ref. Job 22: 28)

They forget that God had set conditions for these to be fulfilled. So if for instance, they do not acquaint themselves with Him as Job 22: 21- 23 instructs as a condition for fulfillment, they could decree "unto eternity" with no results to show. The same applies to the new covenant. If you are not saved, you can lay claim to all the blessings in it even "unto eternity", if that were possible, but with no effect.

A friend of mine while I was in the university had sickle cell disease. He was born with this genetic disorder. He was, as is popularly but erroneously called, a "sickler". This term was coined because of the fact that those born with this disease frequently fell ill with various life-threatening complications. Sickle cell disease is the full-blown variant of a number of sickle cell anaemias, and it is associated with a high fatality rate because of the very severe complications that could arise from it. It is an intrinsic genetic disorder in the red blood cell genotype that results in the abnormal genotype SS. The genotype found in normal individuals is AA. The red blood cells are responsible for the transport of oxygen to tissues of the body. In sickle cell disease, the red blood cells are under certain conditions liable to take a sickle form, and in this form, the transport of much needed oxygen to body tissues is less efficient. This impairment in function can lead to various life threatening complications. Most people with sickle cell disease do not live beyond middle age. Medicine and Science have no answer yet to this genetic scourge.

As far as I had known this friend of mine, he had suffered greatly from this condition. We had been study group partners during my early years in medical school, and I had hardly seen anyone suffer so much health wise and still remain so hopeful even with the rigors of medical school work. He fell from one or more complications of this disorder to another. In one instance, there was a complication of chronic leg ulcer on his right leg that was further complicated by infection of the bone (osteomyelitis). This led to his incapacitation in movement. This condition was further exacerbated by other complications of sickle cell disease, including what we call medically, *"avascular necrosis of the head of the right femur (thigh bone)"*. Avascular necrosis here means death of the head of the femur bone because of a compromise in its blood supply. You see the bone is a tissue, and needs oxygen to survive just as other parts of the body like the brain and muscles. Deprivation of these needs will result in its death.

The condition had also resulted in a pathological fracture of his right hipbone. The condition had become so severe and urgent. He was told by the doctors that the only option of saving his limb was to have a total hip replacement (total hip arthroplasty) done. In this very difficult situation, he insisted he would not have an arthroplasty for his hip, and he anchored his faith on God. He had taken "the risk" of losing his entire right limb by laying claim to the healing he had in the salvation covenant of God. He was left to his own fate by medicine. Science had no answer to the stings of many genetic disorders like sickle cell disease; he was faced with the increasing possibility of not only losing his entire limb, but also dying early from complications of the disease. Where would all the dreams he had so tenderly nurtured and cherished go? Where was God in all these?

You see dear friend, God never said He would heal us. He said He has already done it:

"who himself bore our sins in His own body on the tree, that we, having died to sins, might live for righteousness- by whose stripes YOU WERE HEALED" [1 Pet. 2: 24]

In the new covenant, most of the blessings are in the "past tense." If so, then where are all of such blessings? Scriptures tell us that God has blessed all believers.

"Blessed be the God and Father of our Lord Jesus Christ, who has blessed us (believers) with ALL SPIRITUAL blessings in heavenly places (Grk. **"in the heavens")** *in Christ"* [Eph. 1: 3 (KJV)]

You tap into such blessings **by faith**. These blessings are spiritual and are in the heavenlies. Whenever you come across any verse that has to do with "spiritual", then you must know and understand that you can only tap into and benefit from such by faith. Such blessings as healing, deliverance, gift of the Holy Spirit and even salvation are all spiritual. You cannot see or know the spiritual with your physical senses. You see and know it by faith!

Believers are already blessed by means of the new covenant of which they are partakers. Nevertheless, to enjoy these blessings, you must tap into them by faith. Believers live and walk by faith:

"The just shall live by faith…, for we walk by faith, not by sight" [Rom. 1: 17; 2 Cor. 5: 7]

This friend of mine, having rejected the only seeming hope to salvage his limb, went home and cried out in faith to God. He laid claim to his healing. And God did honour to his faith! Infact, he got more than he expected! In a routine test done on him after that, his genotype was confirmed to be AA, perfectly normal! Now even he could not grasp what was happening. He thought for sure that it was probably a mistake, for he was expecting to receive at most healing for his right limb and not the sickle cell disease. A subsequent test done still confirmed the result of AA. The dwindling lights of his dreams were rekindled; his dying hopes were rejuvenated; his life was now given clearer purpose, all from a single act of God in just one moment. He is now on the evangelistic road. Praise be to God!

My dear friend, a God who can turn an SS, a genetic disorder, into AA can do anything! He has declared,

"Behold, I am the Lord, the God of all flesh. Is there anything too hard for Me?" Jerem. 32: 27

He keeps challenging every believer today with that same rhetorical question. A man might suffer greatly for the better part of his life, but it takes God less than a moment to fix it all up perfectly and render him a double portion of all he had lost. Job had suffered long, but it took God just a moment to restore a hundredfold all that Job had lost (Ref. Job 42: 10- 17). This only comes by receiving Jesus into your life as Lord and Saviour and tapping by faith into your rightful blessings as a partaker of the covenant with God.

Chapter 4

Unconscious Man
Miraculously Healed

*M*ore dimensions to the workings of God were opened up to me during my clinical years in medical school. In one of such instances during my fourth year, I and some brethren in my local church visited a hospital to share the gospel of Christ Jesus and pray for the sick. I met a patient, a young man, who was involved in a road traffic accident and had sustained severe head injury. He was admitted as a neurosurgical case and had been unconscious since he was admitted. When I met him, he was obtunded and disoriented in his speech, and there were some hemorrhages in his right eyes. I turned to his brother and began to share the word of God with him. I remember the word I shared with him was on the need for him to only believe God, taking this from the story of how Jesus raised up the daughter of Jairus from the dead (ref. Mark 5: 22- 43). After sharing this gospel with him, his faith was stirred up to receive the miraculous from God.

Now a note for believers who go out to pray for the sick- never lay your hands and pray for the sick without stirring up their faith through the word of God. Praying for a spiritually faithless person is like laying your hands on a stone. Faith is what draws the healing power of God from you into an individual, just as a magnet draws an iron rod to itself. You are a reservoir and vessel of the power of God by the Holy Spirit who lives and operates in and through you. It is what the Apostle Paul calls the law of the Spirit of life in Christ Jesus.

"For the law of the Spirit of life in Christ Jesus has set me free from the law of sin and death" Rom. 8: 2

Notice that he said "in Christ Jesus", meaning that this law operates in everyone who is IN CHRIST JESUS, that is, in believers. The law operating in an unbeliever is the law of sin and death. Believers carry life in them by the Holy Spirit. This is the law that operates in them. They are a walking divine throne. So a believer can lay hands on the sick and transfer this life to them as long as they only believe. Faith is that "osmotic gradient" that is required to initiate the flow. Faith in itself is obtained by the word of God. ^{Romans 10: 17} Besides this, you can however lay hands and pray for the sick if you are under the healing anointing. You see, people get healed by two ways- first, by simple faith in the word of God which was emphasized above; and second, by the action of the healing anointing or the gifts of faith and healings. If the healing anointing is present, you can lay your hands on anyone and get them healed by the power of God. By the gift of faith, the faith of God stands in for the sick, and so when God sees the sick fellow, He sees His faith standing or interceding for them, and they receive their healings. The gift of faith is the faith of God. That is why it is called a gift. It belongs to God and He just gives you a part to function in for a certain purpose and time. The faith of God is unwavering and knows no limit, unlike human faith. It is the faith by which He created the heavens and the earth, and by which He repopulated the earth with living creatures in the Adamic era. This is why anyone operating in this gift can receive ANYTHING from God, no matter how mighty it seems. This is the faith that Jesus referred to which can move mountains.

"So Jesus answered and said to them, 'have faith in God' (Grk. "have the faith of God").

"For assuredly, I say to you, whoever says to this mountain, 'be taken up and cast into the sea,' and does not doubt in his heart, but believes that the things which he says are coming to pass, whatever he says shall be his" ^{Mrk. 11: 22, 23 (EMTV)}

Howbeit, the surest and simplest means of receiving healing is by simple faith in the word of God. There are times you may not feel the healing anointing to minister; the word of God is however ever present.

Now I moved closer to the bed of the unconscious man, I placed my hands on him and prayed for him. At that instant it seemed to me like nothing had happened. I never felt the usual tingling sensation in my fingers that is associated with the anointing; just raw, simple and sincere faith in God's word, using his brother as a point of contact. Back then I never knew as much on healing and the anointing as I do now. I left the bedside and came back some time later. To the glory of God, this young man who had been unconscious with head injury was totally healed. He was well oriented, and the hemorrhages in his right eye were all gone. He never ceased praising God for his healing.

Chapter 5

Acknowledgement

"I acknowledged my sin to You, and my iniquity I have not hidden. I said, "I will confess my transgressions to the Lord," and You forgave the iniquity of my sin" (Psa. 32: 5)

The first thing you must do to receive salvation is to realize or acknowledge that you are a sinner and so in need of salvation. Salvation does not exist for believers but it exists because there are sinners in the world. If there were no sinners in the world, Jesus Christ would not have come. But He came to save sinners, [1 Tim. 1:15] for all in the world had sinned and fallen short of God's glory. [Rom. 3: 23]

It begins by taking a sober look at yourself inwardly. If you have not sincerely given your ENTIRE life to Jesus Christ, then you are still a sinner. It does not matter how nice or religious you are. Some might say, "I do not commit so and so sins; I give more than half my earnings to the poor, I do not steal, I do not tell lies, I fast three times a week, pray every hour, I have never indulged in fornication or sexual immorality my entire life and such like there." Very good track record. But for as long as such people have not received Jesus into their lives, they are still sinners and must realize they are sinners in order to be saved.

Man was never a sinner because of the personal sins he committed; neither is man righteous or justified before God because of his good works. Man became a sinner because of the sinful nature transferred "spontaneously" to him from Adam, for as *"by one man (Adam) sin entered into the world, and death by sin; and so death passed upon all men, for all have sinned,"* Rom. 5:12 *"...and fall short of God's glory."* Rom.3:23

So a man who has never personally sinned in his entire life but has not received Jesus into his life is still condemned to hell. Moreover, man's righteousness are as filthy rags before God. Isai. 64: 6 Only in Jesus Christ is salvation found. Acts 4: 12 God is so holy that His eyes are too pure to behold iniquity. Hab. 1: 13 God had previously made a covenant with Abraham Gen. 15: 17, 18 but before He could establish it with Abraham, He gave him the condition to walk before Him and be flawless. Gen. 17: 1 This condition was given to Abraham at a very old age- when he was ninety nine years old. As Abraham kept his part of the "deal", the covenant was effected and his reward was exceedingly great. Gen. 17: 4- 8 So age was and is still no barrier or excuse for any man to live as a sinner before God.

When God Almighty revealed Himself to the Prophet Isaiah, the prophet on beholding God took an honest look at himself and realized how sinful he and his people were. Isai. 6: 5 Before now he had lived so unaware of how sinful he was. He must have thought that he was righteous and blameless, and must have thought the same regarding his people. But infact they fell far short of God's required standards for them. The prophet only realized this when he saw the most holy and perfect God. Before he could even speak to the Lord, his iniquity had to be taken away and his sins purged by a live coal placed on his mouth by one of the seraphim that ministered to God. Observe how the Prophet Isaiah <u>realized</u> how sinful he and his people were, confessed it and his sins were purged and his iniquity taken away. Isai. 6: 6- 7 God only began to speak to him when his iniquity was taken away. He eventually became an extraordinary instrument in the hands of God.

Only the righteousness of Jesus can make anyone stand before God and communicate with Him without guilt. It is this righteousness that gives one access to the throne of the Most Holy God. This righteousness is imputed to a sinner when he receives Jesus into his life, and whenever God sees such a person, He does not see their own righteousness which are as filthy rags before Him, but rather sees the spotless righteousness of His son Jesus which had been imputed to that person. This is why God made Jesus who had no sin to be sin for us, so that in Jesus we should become the righteousness of God. 2 Cor. 5: 21 In the book of Revelation chapter 5, God holds a scroll in His right hand as He sits exalted on His glorious throne.

A proclamation is then made for anyone worthy enough to approach the throne of God, take the scrolls from Him and loose its seals. The revelation of future events depended on this. No one on this earth, under the earth, or even in heaven where the angels resided was able to open the scroll or look at it. Not even the angels or four living creatures themselves. The only one found worthy to approach God and open the scroll and loose its seal was Jesus Christ, the lamb that was slain. [Rev. 5: 1-7] And it is only this same Jesus that can make anyone worthy to approach God.

Nature of your sins

God came to die for every sinner, not just liars, murderers, adulterers, fornicators and any such sinner. ALL that call on the name of the Lord Jesus (for salvation) shall be saved [Rom. 10: 13] and whosoever comes to Him will NEVER be cast away by Him. [Jhn. 6: 37] No sin is too big for Him to forgive. The blood of Jesus is not too weak to cleanse only some sins. This blood was not shed for anyone in vain; it is all powerful and all cleansing. God is calling,

"Come now, and let us reason together. Though your sins are (so terrible) as scarlet, they shall be as white as snow; though they are as red like crimson, they shall be as wool." [Isai.1: 18]

"Only acknowledge (realize) your iniquity, that you have transgressed against the Lord your God." [Jerem. 3: 13]

The word "scarlet" as used in Isaiah 1: 18 is derived from a deep dye which was produced by certain coccus worms found on the leaves of oak trees in Israel and certain other lands. The deep dye produced by these worms was used in dying clothes and other items. This dye was so strong that once an item was dipped into it only twice, it became permanently stained with the dye and nothing could remove the stain. But God here is calling the sinner to come and sit with Him at a round table and present his arguments or case before Him, just as a loving father would sit down with his rebellious son and give him the opportunity to state his grievance before him and so end the friction between both of them. God also would state his own case before the sinner. By this both parties were reasoning together. The importance of this is for the sinner to depart from sin and turn to God, and God on His part would cleanse the sinner from his sins, notwithstanding how appalling they seem, even if the sinner appeared permanently stained as the deep dye (scarlet) would permanently stain items. No stain is permanent that the blood of Jesus cannot cleanse.

With all humility acknowledge your sins and your need for cleansing and salvation which can only come through Jesus. Jesus in Luke 18: 9- 14 tells the story of two men who went to pray in the temple- one a Pharisee and the other a tax collector. Both men were sinners but had contrasting attitudes to the true state of their souls. While praying, the Pharisee swam deep in self righteousness and never saw any need for personal cleansing. He spoke of his good works as a means of his justification and sanctification- he was not an extortioner, not unjust, not an adulterer, fasted twice a week according to Jewish customs, and gave his tithes regularly. He even made a contrasting comparison between himself and the tax collector, and gladly thanked God for not being like him. The tax collector on the other hand came before God, not in self righteousness but humbly as a sinner. He acknowledged that he was a sinner and so needed the mercy of God. He would not even lift his eyes up to heaven but smote his breast in deep contrition. This man went home justified; he returned with the mercy of God while the Pharisee returned with the judgment of God.

King David who was a man after God's own heart provides another scriptural example of acknowledging sins before God. When David committed the sin of adultery with Bathsheba, the wife of Uriah and devised the murder of Uriah, her husband, [2 Sam. 11] he received condemnation from God through the prophet Nathan. And what did he do? He instantly sought the mercy of God and prayed for a thorough cleansing from the sin committed. [Psa. 51] He neither denied it nor made excuses for the sin but in his stricken conscience and broken heart, he acknowledged them, [Psa. 51: 3] confessed them and repented of them. Truly sorry for his sin, the Lord accepted his plea, forgave him and put aside his sin. [2 Sam. 12: 13]

You must understand that no man that has sin in him will enter the kingdom of God. The word sin here refers not only to committing sins, but also to the spiritual sinful nature which resides in everyone that is not born again. The Apostle Paul enumerated some sins which include

"Fornicators, idolaters, adulterers, homosexuals, thieves, covetous men, extortioners, drunkards, revilers." [1 Cor. 6: 9- 10]

Others include

"Sexual immorality, impurity, inordinate affection (lust), evil desires, covetousness (greed), which is idolatry; lies, anger, wrath, malice, blasphemy,

slander and filthy communication (language) proceeding from your lips." Col.
3: 5- 9

Galatians 5: 19- 21 also says,

"The acts of the sinful nature are obvious- sexual immorality, impurity and debauchery (lasciviousness; strong immoral sexual desire); idolatry and witchcraft; hatred, discord, jealousy (emulations), fits of rage, selfish ambition, dissensions, factions and envy; drunkenness, orgies, and the like."

The Apostle Paul ends with a strong warning that those who live like this will not inherit the kingdom of God. Col. 5: 21; 1 Cor. 6: 10 These are all works of the flesh and no sinner can overcome such things because they are intrinsic to his nature. Those who even attempted to justify themselves before God by observing the Law of Moses could not overcome it and so they remained condemned before God. But those who are born again are justified by Grace rather than by works which in no way can be perfect. Those who are born of God cannot sin (Grk. ***"adunamai hamartano"*** – do not have the ability to sin) 1 John 3: 9 because they have His nature and are directed by the Holy Spirit and not the flesh. What the law could not do (that is, overcome sin) in that it was weak through the flesh, God did by sending Jesus who taking the likeness of the sinful flesh fulfilled all the law's requirements perfectly for us. Rom 8: 3- 4 So those who are in Him (who are born again) have overcome the sinful nature. Rom. 6: 14 Sinners are still subjected to its nature and by extension its works.

As a man dies, so is he forever. If he dies a sinner, he remains a sinner forever and pays the price for his sins which is eternal separation (death) from God Rom 6: 23 in hell and the lake of fire. Salvation first begins with your acknowledgement as a sinner and your need for salvation, for how can one solve a problem when he does not know what the problem is? Pray this prayer with faith and sincerity:

"My dear lord Jesus, I realize now that I am a sinner. I have sinned not only in my actions and thoughts, but also in my nature and I realize I cannot save myself. O Lord, have mercy upon me, a sinner."

Chapter 6

Repentance

"For I will declare my iniquity; I will be sorry for my sin." (Psa. 38: 18) (KJV)

When man fell through sin in the Garden of Eden, he went astray from God. In the same way the generations that followed did same. Every human being had gone astray from God in his thoughts, actions, in every area of his life, and in his very nature, just as a lost sheep goes astray from its shepherd. Each one followed his own evil ways. [Isai. 53: 6] With sin came death, sickness, struggles and every nameable ill in society. It led to broken homes and divorces, crimes like murder and moral corruption.

To receive the mercy of God for your salvation, you must first turn away from sin itself. You must see it as an enemy, the enemy that has brought hurt to you, your family, friends, neighbours and the society in general. Explicitly put, you must repent. Sin offers no good to the one who befriends it. It takes hold of your hands, leads you to eternal destruction, and then leaves you there to your own fate. To repent simply means, "to have a change of mind regarding the sinful life you live." This only happens when you have realized your true state- that you are a sinner and bound for eternal condemnation, and that this state was generated by sin. Once you have realized this, then you say NO to sin by turning your back on it. *When you realize that it is sin that separates you from your creator and that it is what hinders Him from helping you in the struggles you face, from healing your diseases, mending your broken heart, lifting you out of that depressed state, intervening in your families and friends, then you will understand why you must have a change of mind regarding friendship with sin.* [Isai.59: 1, 2] To receive the reward for befriending sin which ultimately is eternal death, [Rom. 6: 23] you must agree with it because according to spiritual principles, two cannot walk together except they have agreed to do so. [Amos 3: 3] God longs so much to be gracious to you, [Isai. 30: 18] to release His mercy to you for your salvation, but you must take the first step by showing Him how earnest you are to be saved from sin and its devastating effects. No offender thrown into jail can receive pardon except he shows remorse for his offences committed. Same is true with God! He earnestly wants to help you overcome all of life's situations, the struggles, unfulfilled dreams, the uncertain future, the deep inner feelings of depression and loneliness that you may mask with a cheerful look. You may wonder if He does not see those tears you shed in secret, the unending cries for His help, the broken heart yearning for comfort, the dying dreams in urgent need of a revival, the gloomy future in need of illumination, and most importantly the dying soul within crying out for salvation. God wants to help you more than you can imagine but He cannot until you let Him. That means breaking off from sin, and until you turn your back on sin, there is absolutely nothing He can do. Your sins may have caused a lot of hurt to you, your family, your friends and even the society without your awareness of it! Whoever has friendship with sin is an enemy of God.

The translation of the word repentance in the Hebrew scripture, **nacham**, is very remarkable. It means "to pant" or "to sigh". This expresses a sense of deep regret for the wrongs which one must have done. However the end of repentance is to turn away from the sinful life (that is, to forsake it), hence the Greek meaning of "to have a change of mind". True repentance is not just regretting the sins you have done. God does not want a sinner to only regret the sins he has committed, but to also turn away from them. It is not repentance to just say, "My Lord God, I regret having committed this sin and I will not do it again." This has to be followed by a conscious turning away from such sin and turning right to God and nothing else. Again, the object of your new focus should be God and God alone. [Acts 14: 15] This is true repentance. It paves the way for salvation to come in. True repentance is NOT salvation! The fact that you truly repent of your sins does not mean you are saved. Repentance only makes a way for salvation to come in and salvation in itself is given by Jesus Christ only. [Acts 2: 38; 3: 19] Many abound who repent of a certain wrong committed but never turn to Jesus. This case was seen in Judas Iscariot. Judas Iscariot was one of the twelve apostles chosen by Jesus and he had attained a level where he had not only become a friend of Jesus, but also a brother. He was part of the ministry of Jesus and they both ate from the same plate. (In the East, anyone that ate from the same plate as another became more than just a friend. He was now a brother and both persons were to see to each other's protection and welfare, even in the face of death. This was what made the offence of Judas very grave). Shortly after betraying his master and brother, Judas Iscariot acknowledged his wrong and regretted it, but he never turned to his master for forgiveness and he was condemned in a very miserable way. [Matt. 27: 3- 8; Acts 1: 16- 19] Compare this with Simon Peter, also another apostle and "brother" of Jesus, who committed the serious crime of denying his master three times. [Mrk. 14: 66- 72] He even swore that he never knew Jesus. His offence was as grave as that of Judas Iscariot. But on acknowledging his wrong, he truly repented of it and turned to Jesus and was saved. Judas only regretted (only had a change of mind) but never turned to Jesus. He kept focusing on his wrongs and feeling sorry for himself. His was worldly sorry that led to his death, that of Peter was a godly sorrow which brought about repentance that led to salvation. [2 Cor. 7: 10] Never remain hooked on to regretting your wrongs but once you have truly repented of your wrongs, confess them and turn to Jesus for mercy and forgiveness. Instances abound in scripture when men truly repented of their sins, while some only just regretted.

Manasseh, the son of Hezekiah, was king over Judah, the southern part of a divided Israel. [2 Chron. 33: 1- 20] His wickedness before God was unparalleled in the history of Israel. His sins were compared to those of the idolatrous nations whom the Lord God had thrown out of the land of Canaan during the time of Moses. Let us take a brief look at the *"résumé"* of some of his sins:

1. He rebuilt pagan (idolatrous) worship places which his father Hezekiah had destroyed [v. 3]

2. He made altars (a place for sacrifice) for Baal (an idol god) and poles for Asherah (a Canaanite goddess).

3. He worshipped ALL the host of heaven (sun, stars, moon and such like there) and served them (cp. Isaiah 42: 8).

4. He went as far as building altars for ALL the host of heaven in the two courts (outer and inner courts) of God's temple [v. 4, 5]

5. He placed a carved image of Asherah, which he had made, in the temple of the Lord.

6. He made his sons to pass through the fire in the valley of the son of Hinnom. That is, he offered them up to his gods as sacrifice by causing them to be consumed by fire in this valley. This was a regular ritual of the most evil kings at that time. If during wartime the battle was not proceeding in their favour, they took up their first sons and offered them up as sacrifice in this manner to obtain favour and victory from their gods. If it still did not favour them, they took the next son in line and again offered him up in a burnt offering. This continued until the very last one that could be offered.

7. He practiced soothsaying, used witchcraft and sorcery, and consulted mediums and spiritists.

8. It reached a point when he seduced his people to do more evil (abominations) than the nations which the Lord had thrown out before Moses and Israel.

9. He shed so much innocent blood, till he had filled Jerusalem from one end to another with them. [2 Kgs. 21: 16] Tradition has it that the Prophet Isaiah, whom God used to give warnings to the people during the reigns of Uzziah, Jotham, Ahaz, and Hezekiah, was one of the victims brutally murdered by Manasseh. He was sliced in two with a saw.

Notice how each sin got progressively worse. God sent warnings to Manasseh and his people to repent because He was unwilling to have them destroyed, but they remained stiff-necked and refused to listen. [2 Chron. 33: 10] Consequently, God never relented in sending destruction their way. Assyrians took Manasseh into captivity. But in his distress, he acknowledged his sins, repented and sought the presence of God by imploration, humbling himself greatly before God and praying to Him. Notwithstanding the horrible sins of Manasseh, God whose mercy is great and endures forever [2 Chron. 20: 21; Psa. 57: 10; 100: 5; 103: 17] and who yearns to be gracious to all men, [Isai. 30: 18] had mercy on Manasseh and restored him back to his place in Jerusalem as king. Manasseh became a changed man and began to serve the Lord God. He instigated religious reforms in Judah- he removed the idols from the temple of God and from Jerusalem as a whole; [v. 15] he repaired the altar of the Lord and sacrificed peace and thanks offerings on it, and he commanded Judah to serve the Lord God. His end was far better than his beginning because he had obtained the mercy of God. He ended up as the longest reigned king of the entire Israel (both Northern and Southern kingdom).

The verdict of man on Manasseh, considering his terrible sins, would have been outright death; but God thought so differently about him despite how sinful he was. He sought every opportunity to show His mercy. He only sent judgment as His last resort after all attempts to draw him back from sin did not avail. God intensely loves every man regardless of who they might be. Everyone, even the sinner, holds a very special place in His heart. That is why He created you in the first instance.

Another instance of true repentance is seen in the penitent thief who was crucified with the Lord Jesus. Jesus was crucified with two criminals and while on the cross, He endured ridicule and invectives from the people He was dying to save. These two criminals who were being justly condemned for wrongdoing also poured invectives on Him. [Matt. 27: 44; Luk. 23: 39] They never understood that the cross was a necessary path He had to take for the salvation of all men to be possible. However, one of the criminals repented and was able to draw a wide difference between Jesus and himself. He realized that they had committed a crime and were punished justly for their crime, but Jesus was being punished unjustly. [Luk. 23: 41] This acknowledgement led to his repentance and right on the cross, his salvation was secured by Jesus with a SURE promise. [Luk. 23: 43]

Luke 19: 1- 10 narrates the story of a man named Zacchaeus who was not just a tax collector, but a chief one at that. He was also understandably rich, [v. 2] as chief tax collectors who had subordinates were in charge of customs collected from goods which were exported out of or imported into the land. They were Jews appointed by the Romans to collect these taxes which in turn were given to Caesar; but most of them overtaxed the people to facilitate acquisition of some gain for themselves, Zacchaeus being one of such, and this accounted for why most of them were deeply hated by their fellow Jews. They were generally regarded as sinners. Zacchaeus was not spared this immense hatred and he was seen as a sinner for this. [v. 7] Regardless of this, his soul yearned for Jesus, as evidenced in his determination to see Jesus at any cost despite his short stature that stood as a hindrance. He humbled himself of his high status in the Jewish society and climbed up a sycamore tree to satisfy the desire of his soul and he got more than he expected- his determination was rewarded when Jesus called him down to dine with him. Zacchaeus was privileged and repented of all his wrongs and gave out half of his goods to the poor. The eventual result was amazing. He and his entire family received the salvation of Jesus. [Luk. 19:]

[9] This was the very thing Jesus came to give to all men, and it was received by a sinner, who irrespective of being despised and rejected, and rightfully so, repented and got more than he bargained for in salvation for himself and his entire family.

The church in the city of Corinth provides another scriptural example of repentance that leads to salvation. The city of Corinth was disreputed for every form of imaginable sin, and was only second to the city of Athens with regards to idolatry and sexual immorality. Consequently the church here had gone astray. There were reports of strife, [1 Cor. 1: 11] sexual immorality (fornication) [1 Cor. 5: 1] at a level that was not even tolerated or found among sinners- a man had taken his father's wife while the father was still living. [2 Cor. 7: 12] Yet he was, even with such sin, warmly received in church without shame! Such a sin was an abomination even to the very immoral sinners in Corinth. Other acts of this church included taking minor disagreements within the church to sinners to judge for them, [1 Cor. 6: 1] divisions in the church, [1 Cor. 11: 18] heresies, [1 Cor. 11: 19] unbelief in resurrection of the dead [1 Cor. 15: 12] amongst others. All these were reported to the Apostle Paul who wrote a heart rending letter to this church- the first epistle to the Corinthians. On receiving this letter, many of those that made up the church at Corinth sorrowed much and this sorrow caused them to repent of their sins and this further led to their salvation. [2 Cor. 7: 9- 12] This was not regret or worldly sorrow which leads to death as was the case of Judas Iscariot, but it was a godly sorrow which caused them to turn their backs on their worldly ways, and so lead to their salvation. Let us now consider an example of a man who never truly repented of his sins and the fate that eventually befell him.

The name Ahab when mentioned in scripture instantly brings the word "sin" to mind. His *"résumé"* in sin was so "fantastic" that scripture tells us he committed more evil in the sight of God than any other king before him did. [1 Kgs. 16: 30] The sins of Jeroboam (the king who was given the cognomen "the man who led Israel to sin") were too small in his sight and too inconsequential for him to practice. He married Jezebel the daughter of Ethbaal, the king of Sidon and priest to Astarte, Phoenician goddess of the moon and female counterpart and consort of their sun god, Baal. Astarte was referred to as the "queen of heaven" in Jeremiah 44: 25. By his marriage to Jezebel, Ahab introduced the gods of these Sidonians to Israel. He did more to provoke God to anger than all the kings before him. [1 Kgs. 16: 33] Spurred on by his wife, he falsely accused an innocent man, Naboth, who had relentlessly refused to sell his vineyard to him. He had Naboth killed so as to possess the man's vineyard. This particular act filled up the cup of his sins and brought forth God's judgment upon him and his entire family through the Prophet Elijah ¹ ᴷᵍˢ· ²¹ On hearing God's judgment upon himself and his family, he tore his clothes in grief, and put on sackcloth on his body. (Sackcloth was a rough cloth made of hair that was worn next to the skin as a symbol of deep sorrow or repentance. It was worn with ashes and never removed, even at night. It is called sackcloth because the rough cloth was usually used to make sacks for storage of goods). Ahab also fasted and lay in the sackcloth and went about mourning. ¹ ᴷᵍˢ· ²¹: ²⁷ How did God react to this? God was really impressed by Ahab's actions! Infact God did not hide it but made it known to his Prophet Elijah and so impressed was He by Ahab's humility and repentance that He suspended the intended judgment upon Ahab to the reign of his son. ᵛ· ²⁹ By this God had shown that for everyone, even as evil as Ahab, His mercy always took priority over His judgment for as long as the sinner was willing to humble himself before Him and repent of his sins. Very sadly however, Ahab's humility and repentance did not last long. Because of the ever present stimulant for sin in his wife Jezebel who stirred him to do evil, he reverted to his old ways and committed sin before God again. This time his case was finally settled before God. He and his family were to be cut off. He died gruesomely on the battlefield and dogs licked up his blood as God had declared against him in judgment. ¹ ᴷᵍˢ· ²²: ³⁴⁻ ³⁸

God showed that despite how terrible a man's sins were before Him, He was always willing to show mercy as long as the sinner acknowledged them, humbled himself and turned from them. He so values and cherishes a sinner that there is great celebration in heaven over one sinner that repents than ninety nine righteous persons that need no repentance. ᴸᵘᵏ· ¹⁵:⁷ The reason is not far fetched- whoever dies a sinner is condemned to eternal torment and separation from God. This is irredeemable! So God urgently calls everyone to repentance for their own good. ² ᴾᵉᵗ· ³:⁹ What sense shall it make enjoying all the world can offer for this short time you live on earth, but then dying in your sins and waking up in hell to the reality that you are to be in torment forever and without hope of salvation or a future, as that in itself is past for you. Then all good times you enjoyed in the world would suddenly neither make sense to you nor find any place in you to relish. Just endless torments! It is only a wise man that ensures his salvation is secure in his pockets before he pursues other things in the world.

If you think you have strayed so far from the Lord and you are right now wandering in a desert that you feel He can not find you, or that your sins are far too terrible for Him to forgive and save you, or you have gone so deep into any sin that He cannot reach out to you, well I have good news for you! There is absolutely no desert where the Lord cannot reach out to you; there is absolutely no sin which the blood of Jesus cannot blot out completely; [Isai. 44: 22] there is absolutely no depth in the sea which the hand of Jesus cannot reach and pull you out. This is one of His specialties! Scripture says that this earth and everything in it belongs to the Lord. [Psa. 24: 1; 50: 10- 11] He created it and so knows every nook and cranny of it. I bet you there is no one who can hide in any place of my house that I cannot find him. Why? Because the building of that house was my whole idea. It was designed to my own taste and recommendations. The same is with God. Read what David says of God in Psalm 139. Considering the infinite knowledge and power of God, he asked the rhetorical question in verse 7,

"Where can I go from your Spirit? Or where can I flee from your presence?"

If he ascended into heaven, God was there. If he made his bed deep in hell, God was there. If he went into the deepest parts of the sea, God was also there. Even darkness is as light before Him. In the earth, there is no hiding from God. [Jerem. 23: 23, 24] He is the Lord, the God of all flesh and there is nothing too hard for Him to do. [Jerem. 32: 27] Repent and clear the path for God's salvation. Declare these to God with ALL sincerity and deep humility in your heart:

"My dear Lord Jesus, I have acknowledged before that I am a sinner. I had never known how harmful my sins had been to my family, my friends, the society and me but now I realize it. If I had the ability, I would have undone all the consequences of my sinful life but unfortunately, I cannot. I am truly sorry for my sinful life and I deeply regret all my sins and the terrible effects they have had on my life and on those around me. I now rest on your infinite mercies. Have mercy on me, dear Lord according to your unfailing love for me! In Jesus' name"

Chapter 7

Confession

"And the seed of Israel separated themselves from all strangers, and stood and confessed their sins, and the iniquities of their fathers" (Neh. 9: 2) (KJV)

Do not confuse this third step of confession with the first step of acknowledgement. Acknowledgement is an inward realization or conviction you have that you are a sinner and in need of the salvation of Jesus. Confession is an outward declaration to God of your state as a sinner. This includes not hiding any wrongs before Him. It is like laying yourself bare before Him and telling Him honestly those areas of your life which are not right before Him. Confession is an open acknowledgement of your sins to your creator. Knowing that there is no sin hidden before His sight, God is especially pleased when man takes the initiative or first step in confessing such sin to Him rather than wait for Him to expose them and pour out His judgment upon him. As God through His Holy Spirit brings your sins to your remembrance, confess them to God, for He has said that the man who covers his sins shall not prosper, but the one that CONFESSES and forsakes them will receive mercy. ^{Prov. 28: 13} Confession brings mercy and keeps away God's dreadful judgment. Every sin demands punishment according to God's law and this punishment is death:

"Behold, all souls are mine; as the soul of the father, so also the soul of the son is mine: the soul that sins, it shall die" ^{Ezek. 18: 4}

God is a righteous judge and is bound to be true to His nature by executing judgment on the sinner. But God also established within His law that the sinner that confesses his sins and forsakes them will receive mercy from Him. Would you rather stand before a judge in a law court and deny any wrongdoing and attempt to argue your innocence even when evidence abound that you actually committed a crime? Or would you in deep humility and contrition accept your wrongdoing and confess them before the judge and plead guilty to the crime committed? Even by natural human reasoning, the judge would act in mercy to the one who acknowledges his wrong and pleads guilty, but to the one who attempts to defend himself even in his wrongdoing, the full judgment of the judge would fall upon him, without mercy.

Jesus has assured that if you will confess your sins, He is faithful and just to forgive you your sins and to wash you completely from all wrongdoing, [1 John 1: 9] by His blood [Rev. 1: 5] which He shed without limit for your sake and by so doing, He then presents you spotless (blameless) before the presence of God with joy which is inexpressible and knows no bounds. [Jude v. 24] It is the blood of Jesus that makes you stand blameless before the Judge (God) in His law court. By confessing your sins before Him, He washes you completely in His blood from all your sins no matter how terrible they may be, and then makes you righteous, and you then receive mercy from God. God has declared that if anyone says that he has no sin, he is only deceiving himself and does not have the truth in him. [1 John 1: 8] Whoever does not have the truth walks in darkness (spiritually). [1 John 1: 6] Darkness signifies ignorance and error, and death [Job 37: 19; Isai. 60: 2] Jesus is the truth, and He is the life. [John 14: 6]

In scriptures, confession has made the difference between life and death in the lives of so many men. While those who tried to hide their sins from God were condemned, those who in deep contrition went down before God and confessed their faults to Him obtained His mercy. With His mighty sword lifted high and ready to strike them down because of their sins, they confessed their wrongdoing to Him. He immediately gave the signal for His sword to be lowered and He stretched out His golden scepter of mercy towards them; they took hold of it and were saved from the sword. To those that remained adamant or gave excuses for their wrongdoings, He withheld His golden scepter to Himself, His mighty sword fell upon them in an unrestrained manner, and they were destroyed.

The very first case of covering sin recorded in scripture was that of Adam, the first man on the restored earth. [Gen. 3: 1- 19; Job 31: 33] After Adam and Eve his woman had disobeyed God by eating of the tree of the knowledge of good and evil which He had instructed them not to, they tried to hide themselves from God's presence as the guilt of their sins had visited them.

God in His accustomed manner came into the garden to have a wonderful time of fellowship with His creation but soon discovered what they had done. In order to vindicate himself Adam pushed the blame to God [v. 12] for putting the woman by his side in the first instance, even though he was present when his wife was being tempted [v. 6] and was the one who received the direct command from the Lord not to eat of the tree. [Gen. 2: 16, 17] He tried to cover his sins by attempting to vindicate himself of any wrongdoing even when he had done wrong. The consequences were far reaching, going down his generations up till this moment. Whoever is not born again (of the Holy Spirit through the blood of Jesus) is naturally a descendant of Adam and is under the curse placed upon him. Jesus Christ took that curse placed on Adam upon himself so that those who believe in Him would not have to pay for the sins committed by Adam anymore.

The next recorded case in scripture of one covering his sins is seen in Cain. [Gen. 4: 3-16] Cain and his brother Abel had brought offerings unto the Lord, and while the offering of Abel was accepted by the Lord, that of Cain was rejected, all for a just reason. Both Cain and Abel were sinners in the first instance because of the sin of their father Adam. So for they and their offerings to be accepted by God, there had to first be a temporary atonement for their sins and for this, blood had to be shed because without bloodshed there is no forgiveness of sins. [Hebrews 9: 22] By offering his flocks, Abel first made atonement for his sins, even though temporary. For this reason, he was first accepted by God and then his sacrifice. Cain on the other hand, never made atonement for himself, but rather brought as an offering, the fruit of the ground wherein there is no bloodshed. And so he was not accepted in the first place. He became very resentful and jealous and this paved the way for sin to come in. This caused him to brutally murder his brother. When questioned by God on the whereabouts of his brother Abel, he covered up his sin by claiming ignorance of where his brother was. He even showed no remorse for what he had done. [v. 9] The consequences of this was further curses upon Cain, [v. 11, 12] including becoming a vagabond and dwelling away from God's presence. [v. 16]

Saul, king of Israel, provides another example in Scripture. The Lord God had given Saul the mandate to completely destroy the nation of Amalek because the sins of that nation had reached its peak before Him. The Amalekites had during the time of the exodus of Israel from the land of Egypt ambushed and attacked them in the wilderness while they were very weary from the journey, and they showed no mercy nor feared God. [Exod. 17: 8- 14; Deut. 25:17- 19] God then swore to annihilate these Amalekites, including infants, nursing child, and even animals, when the Israelites had finally settled in their own land. This responsibility fell to Saul, the king of Israel. [1 Sam. 15:1-21] Saul however disobeyed God and spared Agag, the king of Amalek, and for fear of his men he also spared some animals and took some spoils. This expectedly incurred the displeasure of God who rebuked the actions of Saul through the prophet Samuel. Rather than acknowledge and confess his sin to the ever merciful and gracious Lord before Samuel, he gave excuses for his sin and tried to vindicate himself in every possible way and put the blame on his men. [v. 20, 21] His actions led to the kingdom of Israel being taken away from him [v. 23] and given to David. Furthermore and even worse, the Spirit of God departed from him, [1 Sam.16: 14] he became an enemy of God [1 Sam. 28: 18] and he became a distressed man until the day of his gruesome death on the battlefield. Even his seeming repentant attitude or Samuel's intercession to God on his behalf did nothing to change the mind of God regarding his fate. It was already too late and God had already made up His mind. Saul was irredeemably rejected by God.

God is a God of mercy, not willing that any man should be condemned because of sin, [Jerem. 33: 11; 2 Pet. 3: 9] but a time comes just as in the case of Saul, when God removes His robes of mercy and adorns His robes of judgment. Then it will be too late and no plea whatsoever would avail for that person, even if Moses or Elijah or Abraham were to intercede, just as Samuel did for Saul with persistent tears unto God. [1 Sam. 15: 35; 16:1] He is a very merciful God, but also a consuming fire. [Heb. 12: 29] Let us now consider some examples of those in the Bible who did not conceal their sins but openly confessed them to God and received His mercy.

It was not so long after the Jews who were sent into exile in Babylon had returned to their land in Jerusalem that Ezra was deployed from exile by Artaxerxes, king of Persia also into Jerusalem as scribe and priest for the people. [Ezra 7: 1-6] On arriving Jerusalem, he discovered several acts of the people there which were grave sins before God and which had incurred His wrath. [Ezra 10: 14] These included intermarriage between the Jews who had just returned from exile and the idolatrous people who had been occupying the land ever since the Jews were exiled to Babylon some years earlier. These intermarriages which also involved the Levites and priests, a people specially set aside unto God [Ezra 9: 1-15] led them to commit abominations in the order of the heathen nations which God had destroyed before Moses and the people of Israel. It was also because of these that the Lord had earlier sent them into exile in Babylon, and they were now in great danger of being cast away from His presence once again. On discovering this, Ezra tore his clothes, plucked out the hair of his head and beard in grief, and sat astonished until evening in acknowledgement and repentance. He then got on his knees, spread out his hands and openly confessed the sins of his people to God with weeping and grief. ^{Ezra 10: 1} He also fasted and prayed for the people in a great show of true repentance ^{Ezra 10: 6} and with him, many of the congregation of the people of Israel wept sore in great repentance. ^{Ezra 10: 1} All these were followed up by a conscious turning away from such sins and going back to God- the priests who had married foreign wives gave them up. ^{Ezra 10: 18} These acts of Ezra and the people turned away the wrath of God and the people abode safely in their land. Nehemiah ^{Nehem. 1: 6; 9: 2, 3} and the Prophet Daniel ^{Dan. 9: 4- 20} also provide similar examples.

David provides another example. ^{Psa. 32: 2- 5} He had sinned against the Lord and was initially unwilling to humble himself and acknowledge and confess it to God. He rather concealed it in his heart because he had hoped that the conviction of sin in his heart would die off slowly in some way. This instead brought him continuous pain, anguish and distress. ^{v. 3} He was continually convicted of his sins by God day and night ^{v. 4} and the burden of sin upon him increased until he could bear it no longer. He then acknowledged and confessed them to God, and God showed Himself gracious and merciful unto him. His sins were forgiven and peace returned to his mind and soul.

Having acknowledged your sins, you must confess them. Many acknowledge that they are sinners, but they are unwilling to make confession of their guilt. They attempt to conceal it. They postpone, or try to dispose of the whole subject. They endeavor to divert their minds, and to turn their thoughts from it by work, or by fun, or by any means possible. Sometimes, they are infact successful in this, but only to their own detriment; but, sometimes also, as in the case of David, the trouble at the remembrance of sins becomes deeper and deeper, defeating their peace, and exhausting their strength, until they humbly confess, and only then do their minds find peace. Confession is a prerequisite for receiving salvation.

Chapter 8

Forsake

"How shall we escape if we neglect so great salvation?" (Hebrews 2:3)

To forsake means to give up or leave your sins permanently, never returning to them but returning to God instead in humility and repentance. A sinner is like a lost sheep which has gone astray from its shepherd; a sheep that goes in its own way different from that of its master. ^{Isaiah 53: 6} When a sinner acknowledges his sins before God, repents of them and confesses them, he must forsake them also. He must leave them behind himself and never return to them. The bible tells us that when a sinner forsakes his sinful ways and thought and return to the Lord, He will have mercy and ABUNDANTLY forgive that sinner. ^{Isai.55:7; Prov.28:13} This is God's promise and God can never break His word ^{1 Pet. 1: 25} or fail to fulfill His promise. ^{Isai. 34: 16}

God is full of mercy and He would not have made that very costly sacrifice of giving His beloved Son if He would not forgive and have mercy. Scriptures tell us the story of how the Prophet Jonah was sent to the city of Nineveh in Assyria by God to warn them of His impending judgment on the city because of their sins. The city was notorious for its wickedness and this wickedness had gone up before God Himself. ^{Jonah 1:2} The prophet Jonah reluctantly obeyed because He knew how merciful God was. He knew that irrespective of how angry God was with an individual over his sins, His mercies always prevailed over His wrath. He understood that God was not in anyway quick to destroy a sinner, but waited patiently for them to turn back to Him. When the king of the city of Nineveh heard the message of Jonah from God, he became remorseful. He and his nobles issued a decree throughout the city that every man should repent

49

and forsake his wicked ways and turn to God. They did this with mighty cries unto God, in sackcloth and fastings. ^{Jonah 3:1-9} When God saw their works (that they had turned from their wicked way), He forgave them and relented from sending the disaster that He said He would bring upon them. ^{Jonah 3:10}

Forsaking your sins and turning to God is very necessary in receiving salvation. It is intertwined with and as important as repentance. In his message to the Jews after the miraculous healing of a lame beggar at the beautiful gate in the temple at Jerusalem, Peter admonished them to repent of their sins and turn to God to have their sins forgiven them. ^{Acts 3:19} Repentance and complete forsaking of sins are prerequisites for forgiveness of sins just as acknowledgement and confession are for repentance. You should not only regret your sins and the consequences of them, but you should also desire to forsake them. God will not help you do the repenting and forsaking. You do them yourself and this will show how remorseful and serious you are to receive salvation. It is not God's desire that anyone should perish in hell; ^{2 Pet. 3: 9} He greatly desires to save people but holding onto sin can hinder Him from doing so. ^{Isaiah 59: 1, 2}

The children of Israel in one of several instances chose to serve idols in defiance of their true God. ^{Judges 10: 6} They did evil in the sight of God. As a result, He handed them into the hands of their enemies who oppressed them severely. They cried out to Him at one instance for forgiveness but rather than pardon them, He pointed out their sins to them and told them to turn to their idols to save them. ^{v. 10-14} In their second plea for mercy to Him, they not only acknowledged and confessed their sins to Him but also forsook them and turned to Him. ^{v. 15-16} Note the special effect these actions of theirs had on God- His soul could no longer endure the misery they were going through. ^{v. 16} He was grieved at their sufferings, and this prompted Him to send Jephthah as a deliverer for them (chapter 15). In another of several instances when they resorted to serving idols, God gave a very stern warning to them to repent and forsake their sinful ways as a condition to live,

"Therefore I will judge you, O house of Israel, every one according to his ways" says the Lord God. "Repent and turn from all your transgressions, so that iniquity will not be your ruin.

Cast away from you all the transgressions which you have committed, and get yourselves a new heart and a new spirit. For why should you die, O house of Israel?

For I have no pleasure in the death of one who dies" says the Lord God. "Therefore turn and live!"[Ezek. 18: 30- 32]

Jesus Christ said that no one can serve two masters- you either have God as your master, or you have sin as your master. If you cling on to sin as your master without any desire to forsake it, you cannot concomitantly have God as your master. This example was demonstrated in the new believers in the region of Thessalonica who had to forsake their idols to serve God and this drew much commendation from the Apostle Paul.

"For they themselves report concerning us what kind of entrance we have had to you, and how you turned to God from idols to serve the living and true God" [1 Thess. 1:9]

God really cares about you, but for as long as you meddle with sin, He can do nothing to save you. Not that He is powerless to save, but His holy nature is incompatible with sin. The path to salvation can be likened to a rebellious man having a destination in mind but walking in the wrong path. He then suddenly realizes that he walks on the wrong path (acknowledgement), he changes his mind about continuing his walk in this path (repentance), he openly acknowledges this (confession), then he turns away from that road (forsake) and heads back to the road that leads him to the right destination (salvation). You must understand that even if he deserts the wrong path he could enter another wrong path which ultimately leads to the same wrong destination, which is no different from the initial journey he made. Consequently it is important he not only turns away from the wrong path but also get to the right path to reach his destination. Forsaking sin therefore entails not only turning your back on it, but also turning to God for salvation.

Chapter 9

Believe

"He who believes and is baptized will be saved; but he who does not believe will be condemned." (Mrk. 16: 16)

ow even if you have acknowledged your sins inwardly, repented of them, confessed and forsaken them but do not believe in Jesus, all these things will profit you nothing. The ultimate aim of all these steps is to lead you to salvation in Jesus Christ, and without believing your salvation will never be possible. To "believe" simply means to "have faith in" or "know that a thing is true and consistently remain true". Therefore to have faith in the word of God is to believe that what He has said is true and will consistently remain true, irrespective of divergent human logic, how unintelligible it might sound, or prevailing circumstances which may seem to lend it some form of incredulity. The object of your faith or belief is Jesus and in what He did for you at the cross and this belief must be associated with confession. Confession, this time not of sins but of who Jesus truly is and what He has become to you. This confession is simply a PROFESSION of your faith. So then how do you obtain this faith that brings salvation to you? First, you must understand that you do not have this faith by your own works as a sinner. It is given by God and as such it is His gift to you in order to help you get saved, for

"without faith it is impossible to please God" Hebrews 11: 6

and no one can receive anything from Him, including salvation, without it.

"for by GRACE you have been saved THROUGH FAITH, and that not of yourselves; it is the GIFT OF GOD,

"NOT OF WORKS, lest anyone should boast." Gal. 2: 8, 9

For this reason God has provided a channel by which you can obtain this faith that leads to your salvation. This instrument is His word or the gospel of Jesus Christ which you have come in contact with, for faith comes by hearing and hearing by the word of God. Romans 10: 17 "Hearing" implies contacting the word of God by any means, be it radio, television, in a church service or Christian gathering, by books, tracts and other materials, and such like there. This gospel of Jesus Christ is

"the power of God which brings salvation for EVERYONE who believes (who has faith) …for the just shall live by faith" Romans 1: 16, 17

This gospel which brings salvation is not far from you but is near you, in your mouth and in your heart…..that if you confess with your mouth that Jesus is Lord and believe in your heart (spirit) that God has raised Him from the dead you will be saved. For righteousness is obtained when one believes with the heart and salvation is obtained when confession is made with the mouth. Romans 10: 8-10 He that believes and is baptized will be saved, but he that <u>does not believe</u> will be condemned. Mark 16:16 Confession here refers to <u>open acknowledgement</u> that you now belong to Jesus and that He is now your Lord. It is NOT an inward acknowledgement in your heart but has to be open for all to know that you have now switched camps from that of the devil to that of Jesus Christ. Your lifestyle should also openly speak of this. Anyone decamping from one political party to another does not do it in secret but openly declares his move and gives his loyalty to his new party. In the same way, anyone that sees you should be able to tell that you now belong to Jesus. You **believe with your heart** (inward acknowledgment) and you **confess with your mouth** (open acknowledgement). These two must be synergized to receive salvation in Jesus Christ. God has said that whoever believes in Him (Jesus Christ) will receive forgiveness of sins Acts 10: 43 and be saved. Acts 16: 31 The Philippian jailer, so desperate for salvation, asked Paul and Silas the very pertinent question,

"Sirs, what must I do to be saved?"

They replied,

"Believe on the Lord Jesus Christ, and you will be saved, you and your household." Acts 16: 30- 34

The word of God was preached to him and to his household and by instrument of this word, they believed in God and were saved.

Scripture in Luke 16:19- 31 tells us the story of two men- one was a rich man and the other a poor man called Lazarus. The rich man was one who had everything he ever needed in this world. First, he was clothed in purple and fine linen. Only princes and the very wealthy men of the society then wore purple clothes and fine linen. Such men were of high standing in the society. The second feature of this rich man was that he lived a very luxurious life, not just for once or twice a week, but everyday. He lacked absolutely nothing which his heart desired. In stark contrast, the other man, Lazarus, was a poor and wretched man. The Hebrew word for Lazarus means a destitute or a needy, poor man. And so it was no surprise that he lived out his name on earth. His life was indeed pathetic. He was afflicted not only with poverty but also by offensive ulcers which were often licked by dogs. He also strongly desired to be fed with the crumbs which fell from the rich man's table but his desires were not met. Now after sometime both men died. The poor man was taken into Abraham's bosom in paradise while the rich man ended up in hell. Their conditions were now sharply reversed- Lazarus was now in great comfort and the rich man was now in great torments in hell. So great was this torment that the rich man who had all he needed while on earth now begged for just a drop of water. What really was the sin of the rich man that made him end up in hell? Was it because he was clothed in purple and fine linen? Certainly not. Being clothed with the best clothes is not sin. Or was it the fact that he lived a very luxurious life? Not at all. Having wealth is not a sin before God. So what was his sin that brought such punishment on him? This man while on earth through unbelief never obeyed the word of God which at this time was the law and the prophets. This was his sin which cost him his very soul in hell. He, out of fear for the fate of his brothers on earth, had to implore father Abraham to send Lazarus to preach to them on earth so they would not repeat the same mistake he made and end up in hell with him. Abraham however replied by saying that they should obey the law.

God has said,

"Today if you hear my voice, do not harden your hearts as in the rebellion…"
Hebrews 3:7

The rebellion refers to the act of unbelief towards God which many Israelites displayed during their journey from Egypt into the land of promise. These men were destroyed along the way because of their unbelief. They heard the voice of God and rejected it through unbelief. Today God is calling every sinner through His word and is still giving the same warning as He did then- "do not harden your hearts". Do not reject this call through unbelief. God has sworn, just as He also did then, that such people will not enter His rest. Hebrews 3:11 Such people stand to face eternal torments in hell. In hell, prayers are not answered; tears are not seen; all the achievements acquired here on earth are of no relevance. In hell there is no hope of salvation. The rich man in Luke 16 had all he ever needed here on earth. He gave his body and soul great pleasures, but kept God far away from his life. In hell, all his wealth became unimportant. Believe in the finished work of Jesus Christ for you at the cross and receive Him into your life to be saved. Pray this prayer with FAITH and SINCERITY:

"My dear lord Jesus, I thank you for the sacrifices you made for me at the cross. I confess that You are indeed Lord and I believe that You were resurrected for my justification. I thank you for doing for me what I could not do for myself. I realize that your sufferings and death on the cross for my sins are more than sufficient for my salvation, and so I do not have to work for it. I thereby rest on your finished work for me on the cross and I believe your word concerning it. Thank you Lord Jesus."

Chapter 10

Receive Him

"Then they WILLINGLY RECEIVED Him (Jesus) into the boat, and IMMEDIATELY the boat was at the land where they were going" (Jhn. 6: 21)

*T*he greatest miracle on earth is the salvation of the soul and this is about to take place in your life. Anyone might get any other miracle from God – healing, deliverance, and such like there- and still end up in hell. One can have the manifestations of the Holy Spirit- prophecy, working of miracles, tongues and such like there- and still end up in hell. But no one can receive salvation and still end up in hell except they lose it through backsliding. The Lord Jesus made the very revealing statement in Matthew 7: 22, 23:

"Many will say to Me in that day (Day of Judgment), Lord! Lord! Was it not in Your name that we prophesy, and in Your name cast out demons, and in Your name do many powerful deeds?"

"And then I will profess to them that 'I never knew you! Depart from me you workers of iniquity!'" (CLV)

This greatest miracle comes when you receive Jesus Christ into your life by faith. You become a child of God and an heir to God's throne; for

"As many that received Him (Jesus Christ) to them He gave the authority to become children of God, to those who believe in His name" John 1: 12 (CLV)

After the miracle of multiplying five loaves of bread and two fish, the disciples of Jesus got into a boat at night en route the city of Capernaum while Jesus departed to a mountain (scripture ref- John 6: 1- 21). While in the boat, the sea arose against them because a great stormy wind was blowing. They were at a great risk of sinking and losing their lives in this storm. But in the midst of this terrible storm, Jesus came towards them, walking on the sea, and they were afraid. But they however WILLINGLY RECEIVED Him, and note what scriptures says thereafter- "and IMMEDIATELY the boat was at the land where they were going." Their lives were saved and they reached their destination because they **willingly received Him into their boat**. What if they had not received Him? That would have been an entirely different story today.

Now having acknowledged your sins, repented, confessed and forsaken them, and believed in your heart that Jesus actually died to save you from sin and its consequences, you receive Him willingly into your life. Sin makes the spirit of a man dead, and it brings pain, sorrow, and sufferings and a very heavy burden upon the sinner. But receiving Jesus into your life, you receive a new life, His very own life; your spirit is rejuvenated and the curse and burden of sin is lifted off. More importantly, you are saved from hell.

Receiving Jesus into your life gives you the RIGHT (authority, and not privilege) to call God your father. In other words, you are now "legally" entitled to everything that He has. You do not beg for them, they are yours by right. The blessings of God become yours because you are now His child. How do you receive Jesus into your life? This is done by faith. Jesus said to Nicodemus a Pharisee that a man must be born again to see the kingdom of God. [John 3: 3-4] Being born again is not of the flesh but entails having the Spirit of God dwell in you after you receive Jesus into your life. When you do this, then you are saved. You know this by faith; the Spirit of God confirms this to your spirit and you know this just as you know that you are breathing. Receiving Jesus and being saved is not obtained by being so religious- attending church services regularly, paying tithes frequently, praying and fasting constantly, attending a particular religious denomination, having archbishops as parents and relatives. No religion can save; philanthropy and charitable works can never save, even if you give all your fortune to the poor; not committing sins like lying, stealing or murder cannot save; acknowledging, repenting, confessing or even forsaking your sins does not mean you are saved, even though they are prerequisites for salvation. Cornelius was so religious, yet he was not saved. Nicodemus was a Pharisee- a professor of Theology- yet he was not saved. Mary, the mother of Jesus, despite giving birth to the messiah was not saved. John the Baptist, despite paving the way for the coming of Jesus Christ and being the greatest of all the prophets, was not saved. No one is saved by his works no matter how good they may seem. It is a deception of the enemy to keep a person comfortable in sin and spiritual death, which ultimately hands him a visa to hell. At judgment, God will judge based on principles and not emotions. Receiving Jesus is the only way anyone can be saved. ^{Acts 4: 12; John 14:6}

Salvation cannot be elucidated by human analysis. The Greeks during the time of Paul attempted it but it only amounted to foolishness; the Jews attempted it but it only became a stumbling block to them. Their sin was made yet more conspicuous. The world today in the face of its far-fetched advancement in technology, still do not understand it by such means. No philosophy in this present age can comprehend it. It is foolishness to them, yet very important to escape the wrath of God in judgment. They cannot understand how a human being can be brutally killed on a cross and this brings salvation to the whole world. No human logic can understand it. This is why salvation is a miracle! You know and understand it by faith. Only the Spirit of God can reveal it to a man. The peace of God settles in your heart and the Holy Spirit constantly witnesses this to you.

The Holy Spirit only convicts the sinner of his sins and his need to receive Jesus into his life and be saved, BUT He does not coerce him into receiving the salvation of Jesus. He in this respect adopts a "gentleman" approach. God still respects the freewill of man to act as he pleases and He will NEVER violate it. He created man with it, and He will not take it. Likewise, the devil cannot take it from man. The devil does not coerce any man into hell or to accept him as master. Every man is responsible for his destiny. The time is past when every man had no choice over his destiny, which was under the authority of the devil. This was the period before Jesus Christ came into the world to save man. All roads led to hell at the death of any man. There was no option of salvation then. Even the righteous men of the Old Testament went to paradise in hell at their death-Abraham, Isaac, Jacob, Moses, Joshua, the judges, David, and such like there. Hell then had compartments for wicked men (called *Hades*), a place full of torment, for the fallen angels called *Tartarus*, and for the righteous called paradise. Paradise in hell was a peaceful place. Abraham's bosom was in this compartment ^{Luke 16:22-26} and there was a great gulf between these compartments. When Jesus died, He descended into hell to preach this gospel of salvation (an evangelist in hell) to those in hell and give them an opportunity for salvation which we now have so abundantly but which they never had. The repentant criminal who was crucified with Him also went to this paradise. ^{Luke 23:39-43} When Jesus ascended into heaven, He ascended with them; ^{Eph. 4:8 9} paradise was lost in hell and is now in heaven. So now only sinners go to hell while believers when they die go to paradise in heaven.

No righteous man on earth before this dispensation of grace was worthy of entering heaven without the blood of Jesus. Not even Abraham, a man called a friend of God; David, a man after God's own heart; Moses, one of the mightiest instruments in the hands of God; Joshua, Isaac, Jacob and their likes. All went to paradise in hell at their death. Not one was worthy to enter heaven without Jesus, although scriptures allude to how they really pleased God through faith. ^{Hebrews 11: 4-40} How much more this generation which have greater privileges than those of the Old Testament! If God did not allow men who though never heard the gospel, were called His own friends, and men after His own heart, to enter heaven but first receive Jesus, will He then allow a sinner who hears this gospel but rejects it to enter heaven? The answer is obvious- not even in eternity! I say then, it is much better for a sinner never to hear this gospel at all than to hear it and reject it. At least on the Day of Judgment, he will have an excuse to give the Lord Jesus as to why he was not saved. But what excuse will a man give if after hearing this gospel, he rejects it? So every man on earth is accountable for his fate. God has now given man a choice, an opportunity to live which they hitherto never had.

"*The Grace of God that brings salvation has appeared to ALL men*". ^{Titus 2: 11}

If God made decisions for men, then all men would end up in heaven, and if the devil took decisions for men, then all men would end up in hell. But not all men have ended up in hell; neither have all men ended up in heaven. So neither God nor the devil decides for you where you should spend eternity. You make the decision yourself. Whoever ends up in hell chose to be there, for it is not God's will for anyone to end up there.

God has said,

"*In an acceptable time I have heard you, and in the day of salvation I have helped you. Pay attention! NOW is the accepted time. Pay attention! NOW is the day of salvation.*" ^{2 Corinth. 6: 2}

Do not postpone till tomorrow what you can do right now, for

"How shall we escape if we neglect so great salvation?" Hebrews 2: 3

It does not matter how bad your sins are. This was why Jesus came – to do that which you cannot do for yourself and which others cannot do for you. He came to bring salvation and peace and even more to your life. He is able to save completely those who come to God through Him, because He always lives to intercede for them. Hebrews 7: 25 He is waiting for you to receive Him into your life to seal your salvation. He stands at the door of your heart right now and knocks. As you hear His voice and open the door, He has promised to come in and dine with you. Rev. 3: 20 Pray this simple prayer with faith and sincerity:

"Dear Jesus, I have now understood your saving work for me. I have acknowledged my sins before you, I have confessed and forsaken them, and have believed in your finished work on the cross for me. I cannot save myself from the penalty for my sins. Just as you have promised that you will not cast away anyone that comes to you, I in all humility come to you as the only One that can save me. Forgive me of all my sins; cleanse me of all unrighteousness and save me according to your promise that if I call upon you I will be saved. I now accept you as my Saviour. I receive you into my life as my Lord. Come and dwell in me and work in and through me as you will. I now believe I am saved. Thank You my dear Lord for saving me. In Jesus Name, AMEN!"

Chapter 11

Consecration

"I beseech you therefore, brethren, by the mercies of God, that you present your bodies a living sacrifice, holy, acceptable to God, which is your reasonable service (Grk. "latreia"- to minister unto God, especially by worship)." (Rom. 12: 1)

Finally, having become born again by receiving Jesus into your life, you should consecrate yourself unto Him. To consecrate simply means to devote your entire self- spirit, soul and body- unto Him. As the Scripture puts it, it necessitates surrendering yourself entirely unto God, like one that has been brought to life from the dead (that is, one that is now born again), and surrendering the parts your body as instruments of righteousness unto God; rather than utilizing parts of your body to sin as instruments of unrighteousness. ^{Rom 6: 13} You are to offer your body as a LIVING sacrifice that is holy and acceptable to God, and this is the right way to worship God. ^{Rom. 12: 1} This implies using parts of your body in service to God rather than in service to sin and worldly pleasures. You should please Him in all your actions, words, and thought. John Graham Lake, the great man of God who was popularly known as the apostle of faith once said, *"Sin manifests itself in three ways: **in thought, in acts, in nature**. Salvation is a complete transformation. God takes possession of man, changes his thoughts; in consequence his acts change, his nature is new. A Christian is not a reformed man. He is a man renewed, remade by the Spirit of God, a man indwelt by God..."* (The New John G. Lake Sermons, page 13). This is only possible when you allow the Holy Spirit who now lives in you to work in and through you, for no man can please God by his own strength. It is the Holy Spirit that helps us to please Him. I reiterate for emphasis, IT IS THE HOLY SPIRIT. Your relationship with the Holy Spirit began the moment you were born again. Grow and maintain that relationship by doing the following:

1. Praying daily. In this you receive the power to live for God, please Him and overcome worldly temptations and fleshly lusts, which wage war against your soul, [1Pet. 2: 11] to haul it into hell.

2. Studying the word of God (Bible) daily. His word gives you:

    ❖ Direction. It is a lamp to your feet and a light to your path. [Psa. 119: 105] His word in conjunction with the Holy Spirit will direct you in your everyday affairs. As believers we live in a world of darkness (that is, spiritual darkness) even though we are children of the light. [1 Thess. 5: 5; Eph 5: 8] Jesus said even though we are presently in the world, we do not belong to it. [John 15: 19; 17:16] How then can you see clearly as you wander through this dark world? It is the word of God that is a lamp and light to see through this darkness clearly.

    ❖ Wisdom of God. [Psa. 19: 7]

    ❖ New Life. [1 Cor. 4: 15; 1 Pet. 1: 23; Jam. 1: 18] It is a means of obtaining spiritual and eternal life. It is the "water" referred to in John 3: 5. The other instrumentation being the Holy Spirit.

    ❖ Revitalizes you. [Psa. 119: 50, 93] The word of God itself is living and active. [Hebrews 4:12]

    ❖ Sanctification. [John 15: 3; 17: 17; Eph. 5: 26] It cleanses you and sets you apart for God's service (that is, it makes you holy).

    ❖ Hope and comfort in exigent circumstances. [Rom. 15: 4; Psa. 119: 49]

    ❖ Keeps you from sinning against God. [Psa. 119: 11]

    ❖ Keeps you from destruction. [Psa. 17: 4]

    ❖ Knowledge and understanding. [Psa. 119: 99, 130]

    ❖ Spiritual growth. [1 Pet. 2: 2]

    ❖ Joy to your spirit. [Psa. 19: 8]

    ❖ Produces obedience in you to the will of God. [Deut. 17: 19, 20]

    ❖ Enables effective prayer and engagement in spiritual warfare. [John 15: 7; Eph. 6: 17] The Holy Spirit does not act on nothing but requires a platform or substrate on which to act to produce an effect or result, and the word of God is the substrate on which the Holy Spirit acts. In the recreation of the earth, [Gen. 1] God spoke the word and the Holy Spirit who had before now been hovering expectantly over the waters of the earth (waiting for the word to be spoken) instantly acted on the spoken word of God and brought about the wonderful works of creation as we know them. Before Jesus healed or delivered an individual, He spoke the word and the Holy Spirit acted upon it to effect the miraculous. The anointing of Jesus in a believer is activated or effected by speaking the word. In the same way, before you received the salvation of Jesus, you first received the word of God in your spirit. The Holy Spirit then acted upon it to effect your salvation. Let this same word of God live in you richly. [Col. 3: 16] It is the sword of the Spirit by which He fights your spiritual battles. If you do not have this sword in place in your life for use by the Holy Spirit, how then will your battles be fought?

❖ Faith. [Rom. 10: 17; John 20: 31] Faith is essential if you are to walk daily with God, just as Enoch who was translated without experiencing death did. [Gen. 5: 24] Infact, you need it to please God in anyway [Hebrews 11: 6] and anything that is not done in faith is sin. [Rom. 14: 23] Prayer is the power that generates the electricity; faith is the transformer that converts the electricity into concrete, visible forms that are beneficial to us. Prayer needs faith to obtain what it desires and faith needs prayer to give it a foundation on which to operate. Even God in the dateless past created the heavens and laid the foundations of the earth by faith. [Heb. 11: 3; Job 38: 4- 7; Psa. 33: 6] Now that you are born again, you are one and the same with your Father in heaven. You live by the same principles. You live, and stand, and walk by faith, not by sight [Rom. 1: 17; Rom. 11: 20; 2 Cor. 5: 7] or your physical senses, because the things which are seen (by the physical senses) are temporary but the things which are not seen are eternal. [2 Cor. 4: 18] With faith, nothing is impossible. Archbishop Benson Idahosa used to say that if your faith says yes, God will never say no. There is so much that can be said about the indispensability of faith to the believer, but the key point is this- faith comes by contacting the word of God, either by hearing or studying it.

3. Sharing Jesus with someone everyday. This is called evangelism. It means spreading the GOOD NEWS of Jesus Christ which has come to all men, irrespective of tribe, sex, religion, location, or status. The ultimate aim of evangelism is to win sinners to Jesus. Jesus has done a wonderful thing for you by saving you and enthroning you with Himself in heaven and so making you a joint heir to the throne of God. Can you afford to be silent about it, and not invite sinners to come and freely enjoy this privilege bought for them by the precious blood of Jesus? Certainly not! They need to hear this good news.

4. Fellowship with your brethren. This is meant to encourage and strengthen you in the faith. As iron sharpens iron, Prov. 27: 17 so do brethren sharpen brethren. Our Lord Jesus Christ admonished us not to neglect the meeting together of our brethren. Heb. 10: 25 Attend a good bible believing and Spirit-filled church near you.

It is God's desire to use every one of His children to carry out His work here on earth. But He needs a consecrated heart; a heart which is set apart or dedicated to Him. A consecrated heart is separated from the world and dedicated to God. The world is an enemy of God and whoever befriends it pushes God aside, because no one can serve two masters concomitantly. You can never be fully dedicated to both of them simultaneously. Friendship with the world makes you an enemy of God. Jam. 4: 4 The sins in the world fall into three categories- the lust (desire; yearning; hunger) to gratify the flesh (carnality), lust of the eyes (or desire for possessions), and the pride of life (worldly arrogance). 1 John 2: 16 These are all this world can offer any man. A mind which is dedicated to the world is therefore an enemy of God. It was for these reasons that Adam fell in the Garden of Eden. God admonishes us to set our minds on the things above (which are heavenly and spiritual) and not on the things of the earth Col. 3: 2

DECISION FOR CHRIST ON RECORD

On this day, I have read this book and I have sincerely taken all the steps for my salvation. I have acknowledged my sins, I have confessed, repented of and forsaken them; I have also believed that Jesus died for my sins and was raised from the dead for my justification. I have received Him into my life as my Lord and Saviour, and I know I am saved. My sins have been forgiven me and blotted out completely just as Jesus promised He would. I am now a child of God and have the Holy Spirit living in me.

I trust that my Lord Jesus who has started this wonderful work in me will see it to completion until the day of His coming. I pledge this day to serve Him faithfully, to run my course to the end, and never go back on my faith. I record these on this day:

DATE:

SIGNATURE:

CONGRATULATIONS! Beloved, you are now a child of God. Whenever you are made to doubt your salvation or your status as a child of God, you can refer to this record which you have made this very day. Do you know what? Heaven is right now in great celebrations because of your decision for Jesus Christ. They had eagerly awaited this moment.

Personally write or e-mail me to tell of this miraculous work that God has done in your life. For every letter or e- mail received, a special prayer is made for you and your loved ones. I keep praying for you and everyone that reads this book. You cannot afford to miss the wedding feast of Jesus in heaven!

Chapter 12

A New Life

"For in Christ Jesus neither circumcision availeth anything, nor uncircumcision, but a new creature" (Gal. 6: 15)

Now that you are born again, you do not now have to work to justify yourself before God, or to receive some blessings from him. You are already <u>complete in Him</u> (Christ Jesus) who is the head of all principality and power; for in Him ALL THE FULLNESS of the Godhead dwells in bodily form. ^{Col. 2: 9} He has blessed you with EVERY spiritual blessing in heaven, ^{Eph. 1: 3} and His divine power has given you all things that you need for life and godliness (true worship). ^{2 Pet. 1: 3} Just let your finite mind attempt to think of every blessing that God can bestow on anyone in heaven, then know for sure that God has blessed you with all of them! There is absolutely NO blessing that He can give anyone in heaven, much less earth, which he has not given you. He will not give you but has already given you because by becoming saved through Jesus, you are now His child and you are entitled to all that He has. You do not ask for them; they are yours for the taking! Let us now consider some of the benefits which you have in Christ Jesus now that you are born again.

1. **Righteousness.** This means the state of being upright or blameless in every aspect of your life. You are made righteous before God not by your works, but by faith in Jesus, because God made Jesus who had no sin in Himself to become sin for you so that in Him (Jesus) you might become the righteousness of God. ^{2 Cor. 5: 21} The righteousness of any man obtained by works is unacceptable in God's sight. They are as filthy rags to Him. ^{Isai. 64: 6} Only this righteousness of Jesus which He

imparts to you when you believe in Him and in His finished works can make you blameless before God. There is nothing more for you to do. What Jesus did for you at the cross was more than enough to make you righteous. Jesus is called the Righteousness of God, [Rom. 3: 21] and this righteousness was God's gift to you the moment you became born again. Once you believe in Jesus, He clothes you with this righteousness. [Rom. 3: 22, 28, 30] A man

"*is not justified (declared righteous) by his works…but by faith in Jesus Christ…for by works no flesh shall be justified*" [Gal. 2: 16]

Now that you are born again, know this, you have the righteousness of Jesus in you!

2. **Sanctification.** To sanctify means to make perfectly holy, something that was previously defiled. In the Old Testament it meant to set something or someone apart for God's use ONLY. For this to be done, such a thing or person had to be purified (cleansed). Sanctification is not just attained in a moment; it is a process. It is the work of the Holy Spirit in a believer in bringing his WHOLE MAN- spirit, soul and body more towards the perfect and sinless state that was commenced in the spirit of the person at the time they became born again. [1 Thess. 5: 23] No man is without sin. If any man says he has no sin, he deceives himself and the truth is not in him. [1 John 1: 8] The inner man (spirit) of the believer is sanctified at the time of his regeneration (rebirth; born again), [1 Cor. 6: 11] but the body and soul too must follow to make the sanctification process complete. *As such a believer must yield to the Holy Spirit continually in bringing his soul and body under the subjection of God. As the believer does this, he becomes more sensitive to sin and becomes more like the perfect Christ Jesus.* Regeneration is the beginning of the sanctification process. Perfect holiness is the end of it. The life of the believer goes in this direction- cleansing by water (the word of God) [Eph. 5: 26] and the blood of Jesus, [1 Jhn. 1: 7; Rev. 7: 14] then justification (righteousness), and then sanctification. Now that you are born again, you are being sanctified by the Holy Spirit to be presented blameless before the throne of God. [Jude v. 24; 1 Thess. 3: 13]

3. **Purification (Cleansing).** God does not use everyone or everything as His vessel, even though He desires to. He uses only those who are cleansed (by the blood of Jesus Christ and the word of God) and made righteous. That is why He is called a Holy God. [1 Pet. 1: 15, 16] Every vessel set apart for God's use in the tabernacle of Moses had to first be purified by the sprinkling of the blood of an animal upon it. [Exod. 29: 21] This blood signified the blood of Jesus which was to be sprinkled upon ALL men who would believe in Him. Only after Moses sprinkled (or cleansed) such vessels with blood of the animal was it then fit for God's use. God is a glorious and majestic king who does not accept just any vessel for His use. He only accepts high standards and this is always his principle. Only purified vessels can be sanctified (set apart) for His use. This purification only comes about by faith in Jesus Christ. [Acts 15: 9] Once you believe in Jesus Christ, you are cleansed by His blood, saved and set apart, and thus meet the qualification to be used as His vessel for honour. More importantly, vessels used by God were to be used by Him and Him only. Any vessel that is cleansed means that it is now the SOLE property of God. It is now holy and set apart for God alone. So once cleansed by faith in Jesus, you become the SOLE property of God. **Your spirit, soul, and body now belong to Him alone, and you no longer use them for the pleasure of the devil or the world.** You live for the one to whom you are indebted-God. The moment any vessel which had been set apart for God's use was used by another person, it instantly became unclean and unfit for God's use, and had to be purified again by blood to become fit for God's use. If you fail in this respect, the blood of Jesus can cleanse you and make you fit again for God's use. As you believe in the Lord Jesus and rest on His finished work on the cross, you are set apart and made fit for God's use. [Heb.10: 10]

4. **Spiritual life.** A life of sin is associated with spiritual death. Every man is a tripartite being made up of spirit, having a soul and living in a body. When God created man, man was a product of THE WORD OF GOD and THE HOLY SPIRIT. God spoke the WORD and the HOLY SPIRIT gave life to man. [Gen. 2: 7; Job 33: 4] Man now had a spiritual life. He was

perfect at this creation. However when Adam first sinned in the Garden of Eden, his spirit man died, for God had warned him beforehand saying,

"...in the day that you eat of it (of the tree of the knowledge of good and evil of which God had commanded him not to eat), you shall surely die." Gen. 2: 17

His soul now took charge and he became more self conscious than God conscious. It is the spirit man that connects one with God. With the death of the spirit, the network was cut off. But Jesus came to give life to every man, and for them to have it till it overflows. John 10: 10 Just as man when perfectly created by God in the Garden of Eden was a product of the Word of God and the Holy Spirit, so is every believer in Jesus Christ (who is born again) a product of the Word of God and the Holy Spirit. Jhn. 3: 5 Every believer is spirit just as man when created in God's image and likeness and in perfection was spirit. This spiritual life is given by faith in Jesus Christ, John 20: 31 for if Christ is in you, even though the body is dead because of sin, the spirit is alive because of (His) righteousness. Rom. 8: 10 The body is dead in the sense that it is no longer responsive to the things of the world. It is no longer an instrument of sin but now an instrument of righteousness for God. Rom. 6: 13 This is the mark of a believer- death of the body (flesh) and life in the spirit.

Why is the body dead? Sin required death as its penalty Ezek. 18: 4 and condition for freedom. Man could not pay this penalty and still live to enjoy freedom. So Jesus the Son of God was sent to take the place of man by paying this penalty of death. This was by crucifixion on a cross. And so to you that believe in Him, when Jesus was crucified on the cross, God saw you as the one being crucified because Jesus was not being crucified for Himself (He had no sin in Him that He should deserve death) but He was representing you on that cross. When He was buried, God saw you as the one being buried; and when He resurrected God saw you as the one being resurrected. And when He ascended on high Eph. 4: 8 and was enthroned in heaven, Eph. 1: 20, 21 you were also taken up on high and made to sit in heaven with Him. Eph. 2: 5, 6 This is the mystery that the world cannot understand. Jesus did not die for Himself; He did all that for you. He represented you on the cross. He did for you what you could not do for yourself. Now when man is crucified, it is his body that is put to death and not the soul, for no man can destroy the soul except God. Matt. 10: 28 Thus on the cross your body was put to death. But you are alive because you were resurrected a spiritual man, by the Spirit of God that dwells in you when you believed in Jesus, for

> *"if the Spirit of God who raised up Jesus from the dead dwells in you,...God will give life to your mortal bodies through His Spirit who dwells in you"* Rom. 8: 11

Jesus died a physical man (that is, His body was put to death on the cross), but He was raised a spiritual man (that is, He no longer depended on the physical body for survival. He did not live for the flesh. His life was now spiritual- dead to the body, alive to the spirit). This spiritual life is a life of faith. It is the life of Jesus given to all who believe in Him. Gal. 2: 20 Jesus, who was the last Adam, became a life- giving spirit unto everyone that believes. 1 Cor. 15: 45 Now that you are born again, know for sure that you have the life of Jesus Christ in you. Live and walk in this consciousness everyday of your life.

5. **Access to God.** When man sinned and died spiritually, his access to God was cut off. Then in order to contact God, man needed an intermediate which was the high priest. Consider this illustration- to have access to or audience with a king, you have to go through certain protocols customarily. You do not just barge in to his throne room to seek audience with him. But suppose the king gave you the privilege of entering his throne room at any hour of the day without interference? The benefits you stand to gain are much more than if you had to follow protocols, not even certain that you would see the king. This was the state of man before and after he sinned. The day he sinned, that access was blocked. The protocols to have audience with God, the greatest king became more difficult. The hindrance was sin. Whoever broke that protocol, coming into His presence with sin, was instantly destroyed. If sin could be properly put out, then that access would be

restored. God had no choice in doing this. He is holy and being principled, He cannot break His word which says that He is too Holy to look upon sin, ^{Hab. 1: 13} let alone interact with it. He hides His face from sin. Even His own beloved Son, Jesus, was not spared as He turned His face away from Him on the cross the moment He saw the huge load of sins of the world placed upon Him. This separation between God and man was symbolically marked by a veil in the temple of God at Jerusalem which separated the Most Holy Place (which was symbolically where the throne of God was) from the outside. When Jesus, the perfect sacrifice, was offered to atone for the sins of man, that veil was broken ^{Matt. 27: 51} and He made it possible for every believer to regain that direct access to God which was lost through Adam. So now, every believer has access with confidence to come into the very throne room of God. ^{Eph. 3: 12; 2: 18; Rom. 5: 2} This is only possible through Jesus Christ. He is the only way to throne of God. ^{John 14: 6; Heb. 10: 19- 20} Now that you are born again, know this surely, you now have direct access to the very throne room of God. Why not enjoy your time having that special audience directly with Him, anytime, anywhere and unhindered.

6. **Spiritual light.** Light metaphorically connotes understanding. When you are born again you receive understanding of spiritual things. You are now spiritual as God your Father is spirit. ^{Jhn. 4: 24} You were born again, not by flesh and blood as in your first birth to your earthly parents, but now by the Spirit of God. A father naturally passes on his traits to his child. In line with this, you have the traits and characteristics of God. God is spirit, so are you spirit living in a body. Spirit interacts with spirit at a spiritual level, just as flesh interacts with flesh at a worldly level. The natural man (worldly man; one who is not born again) cannot understand the spiritual because he does not have the spirit of God. ^{1 Cor. 2: 14} He is not born again. You who are born again can understand them because you have God's Spirit living in you. God works at the spiritual and no man can understand the things of another man except the spirit of the man himself. ^{1 Cor. 2: 11} You can only know what someone else is thinking if he puts his spirit into you. It is his spirit that reveals it to you. God has put His Spirit in all

believers, and so every believer can understand the things of God which are spiritual because God's Spirit living in them reveals and explains it to them. The spiritual level is far higher than that of the natural (worldly) level and it determines the events that occur in the natural. So, a believer at the level of the spiritual has the benefit of influencing events in the natural since he understands the spiritual. Also, the natural cannot understand the spiritual even though the spiritual can understand the natural. So a believer with spiritual light or understanding can judge a natural man, even though the natural man cannot judge a believer with spiritual light.
2 Cor. 2: 15

Light also figuratively signifies direction. Jesus said that every believer is the light of the world. Matt. 5: 14 The unsaved souls are in spiritual darkness Rom. 2: 19; Jhn. 12: 46; 1 Jhn. 1: 6 and in order to find the right path to salvation, we must be a light to them. Jesus, our Lord, came as a light unto this world of darkness, in order to draw men unto salvation through faith in Him. John 12: 46 No servant is greater than His Lord. Jhn. 13: 16 Jesus expects us to do the same. This spiritual light comes when you are born again through faith in Jesus. Jesus is the light of the world, Jhn. 8: 12 and for as long as He lives in you through His Holy Spirit, you have this light in you. Now that you are born again, always walk in this consciousness. Jesus has commanded that believers should let this light

"so shine before men..." Matt. 5: 14- 16

One attribute of light is that it cannot be hidden in darkness. Employ this light to draw the unsaved souls unto salvation in Jesus Christ by your good works.

7. **Adoption.** This means placing someone as a child who is not so by birth. Now that you are born again, you are an adopted child of God. Jesus Christ is the only begotten son of God. Jhn. 3: 16 Believers are adopted children of God. One particular feature of adopted children was that they had equal rights and privileges (including right as an heir) as the children born naturally into a family. In other words, whatever privileges are entitled to Jesus Christ our Lord, applies to you as a believer. How did this adoption come about? To as many as received

(Grk. "obtained") Him (Jesus), to them He gave authority to become children of God. ^{Jhn. 1: 12} How is it obtained? By faith; for you are all children of God, through faith in Christ Jesus. ^{Gal. 3: 26} Now that you are an adopted child of God, you are entitled to the following benefits:

❖ You are under the care of God, just as a loving father cares for his child and supplies his needs. ^{Luk. 12: 27- 33} God has promised you that He will NEVER leave you nor forsake you, ^{Heb. 13: 5- 6} to provide ALL your needs according to His riches in glory by Christ Jesus. ^{Php. 4: 19; Heb. 12: 5- 11}

❖ You are called by His Name, just as a child answers the name of his father. The Name of God opens doors. It is a great privilege for us and a great act of love from God towards us. ^{1 Jhn. 3: 1}

❖ You are conformed to His likeness. ^{Php. 3: 20- 21; Matt. 5: 44, 45, 48; Eph. 5: 1}

❖ You are under His love. ^{Jhn. 17: 23}

❖ You have God's Spirit dwelling in you. ^{Rom. 8: 14- 16} It is the Spirit of God (Holy Spirit) that identifies us as the children of God. He confirms it to us that we now belong to the family of God. It is because of the Holy Spirit dwelling in us that we have the confidence to call God our Father.

❖ You have health. This was secured by the sufferings of Jesus Christ for your sake. Sickness was a result of the sin of Adam, and this curse of sickness was taken by Jesus through His sufferings so that EVERY ONE that lives in Him would enjoy health. ^{1 Pet. 2: 24; 3 Jhn. v. 2; Matt. 8: 17}

❖ Fullness of the Holy Spirit. ^{Jhn. 7: 38, 39; Jhn. 1: 16}

❖ You receive the gifts and fruit of the Holy Spirit. ^{1 Cor. 12; Gal. 5: 22, 23}

Now that you are born again, you are now adopted into the family of God. You are His child and know that whatever belongs to Him rightly belongs to you. It is your right as His child.

8. **Eternal Life.** Death does not mean cessation of all life. Death simply means a separation of something from another thing

which sustains it. It could be physical, spiritual or eternal. In physical death, the inner man (spirit and soul) is separated from the outer (visible) man (hence the name "physical"). In this case, the individual still lives (as spirit) but his physical body no longer exists. Spiritual death is separation of one's spirit from that of God. It does not mean that the individual's spirit no longer exists. The spirit is dead because it is SEPARATED from God. When man sinned in the Garden of Eden, he instantly died spiritually but he lived physically at least for some time. Jesus Christ has given every believer the gift of spiritual life. Eternal death simply means eternal separation from God. Such eternal separation occurs when an individual who is spiritually dead dies physically (that is, when a sinner dies in his sins). So, one who is spiritually dead can be saved for as long as he is physically alive. The moment he dies physically in his sins, he transits into eternal death which is irredeemable. Spiritual death can be temporary but eternal death is permanent. The opposite of eternal death is eternal life and Jesus Christ has given every believer eternal life. Just as death means separation of a thing from its source of sustenance, life means union of a thing with its source of sustenance. Whoever has spiritual life has eternal life. This eternal life comes only by having faith in Jesus Christ. [Jhn. 3: 15, 16, 36; 6: 40, 47] Now that you are born again, the wrath of God no longer remains on you, but you now have eternal life. [1 Jhn. 5: 13]

9. **Gift of the Holy Spirit.** Now that you are born again, you are entitled to receive the Holy Spirit for service. This is called baptism in the Holy Spirit. This is the power of the Holy Spirit coming upon you to qualify you and enable you accomplish the work of God effectively. It is commendable to be zealous for the work of God, but attempting to realize God's work without the empowerment of the Holy Spirit takes you nowhere. It is working by the flesh as opposed to the Spirit, and no man can prevail working by the flesh. [1 Sam. 2:9] When by God's intervention the exiled Jews in Babylon were given permission to return to Jerusalem and rebuild their walls and temple, they returned to Jerusalem and with so much zeal set out to rebuild their walls and temple. They however faced

stiff opposition from some people who never wanted the wall rebuilt and the temple restored. Many became discouraged and were about to abandon the work. But God revealed to Zerubbabel (the governor of the city at this time who was at the forefront of this rebuilding process) through His prophet Zechariah the secret of success in His work- not by man's strength, power, zeal, wisdom, knowledge, oratory, but by His Holy Spirit. Zech. 4: 6 This same secret relates to you as a believer. Every work of God done by the Holy Spirit through you is acceptable to God. The constructors of the tabernacle of God in the time of Moses, Bezaleel and Aholiab, had to be specially anointed with the Holy Spirit by God to be qualified to perform their task of constructing the tabernacle to God's specifications Exod. 31: 1- 6 Similarly, the artisans responsible for making the garments of the High Priest were anointed with the Holy Spirit. Exod. 28: 3; Exod. 31: 6

Jesus Christ is the one who gives this baptism to believers. The Holy Spirit is the instrument. The death of Jesus Christ was necessary to secure the release of the Holy Spirit from God the Father unto Himself. On His resurrection, He as a High Priest ascended into heaven right to the very throne of God with His blood which He shed for the salvation of the world. On presenting the blood to God the Father, He requested the release of the Holy Spirit unto Him. He was the only one qualified for this and His blood cleansed every believer from sin and so qualified them to receive the special gift of the Holy Spirit. Remember the Holy Spirit is first and foremost HOLY and so the cleansing nature of the blood of Jesus is absolutely necessary. On receiving the Holy Spirit, Jesus Christ then poured Him out among believers ABUNDANTLY. Titus 3: 5, 6; Acts 2: 33 Just as the Holy anointing oil when poured on an individual in the old covenant qualified him for a particular office or service, so does the Holy Spirit when upon an individual qualify him to do the work of God.

So, there are three relationships of the Holy Spirit to any human being. First, the Holy Spirit outside and beside the individual. This is the phase of the unbeliever. The Holy Spirit is outside and beside him to convict him of sin because he does not believe in Jesus Christ. [Jhn. 16: 8, 9] Second, the Holy Spirit within the individual. This is the phase of being born again. When a convicted unbeliever receives Jesus Christ into his life and becomes saved, the Holy Spirit moves from residing outside him to dwelling within him. Such unbeliever then moves to this phase. This is the phase of sonship or adoption as a child of God, and it is the Holy Spirit now within this believer that ministers the truth of his sonship to him. [Rom. 8: 15, 16] Third, the Holy Spirit upon the individual. This is the phase of enduement with power for service which Jesus promised the disciples and all believers when the Holy Spirit came upon them. [Acts 1: 8] The disciples at this time had the Spirit of God in them, [Jhn. 20: 22] signifying sonship and adoption into the family of God, but they were not yet empowered and qualified for service. They had to be baptized to function effectively as ambassadors of Jesus Christ earth. Observe the amazing results of this enduement with power of the Holy Spirit on the disciples. Peter who forty nine days earlier had in utter pusillanimity denied and swore ever knowing Jesus, was now able to win souls for his master- about three thousand souls in a day. [Acts 2: 41] Signs and wonders now became a consistent part of the ministry of the disciples and they were able to work for God in the face of stiff opposition because they were never working by their flesh, but by the power of the Holy Spirit.

Our Lord Jesus Christ did not just come to save sinners. He also came to set a standard in life for every believer to attain. He was NOT God when on earth, but a human being. A full fleshed human being like you and me!

*"Let this mind be in you which was also in Christ Jesus: who, being inherently in the form of God, thought it not robbery to be equal with God: but made Himself of no reputation, taking the form of a servant, and **was made in the likeness of men: and being found in fashion as a man**, He humbled Himself, and became obedient unto death, even the death of the cross"* [Php. 2: 5- 8]

Now what would make a man calm a storm, raise the dead, heal every manner of disease, exorcise evil spirits, walk on water and do much more wonderful things on earth? That is the standard He set for every Christian to not just attain but to also constantly and on a daily basis, live and walk in. HIS SECRET WAS THE HOLY SPIRIT. He could do absolutely nothing without the Holy Spirit. The early disciples were able to face horrendous and unimaginable tortures and deaths for the sake of the gospel of Jesus because of the strength and comfort of the Holy Spirit. If our master needed the Holy Spirit to carry out His work here on earth to completion, then every believer is no exception! There is no other way. No servant is greater than his master.

You receive this gift by asking in faith. You do not work for it; you just ask in faith and receive it. That is why it is a gift. It is for you. It is for every believer.

10. **The Gifts of the Holy Spirit.** These are special endowments given to believers by the Holy Spirit to profit everyone. [1 Cor. 12] They come with the baptism or gift of the Holy Spirit. They include revelation gifts (word of wisdom, word of knowledge, and discerning of spirits), vocal gifts (prophecy, different kinds of tongues, and interpretation of tongues) and power gifts (healings, working of miracles, and faith). These gifts are obtained by asking in faith. You do not work to obtain them- you do not fast or do some religious work to obtain them. They are given by grace, not by works; and they are for you now that you are born again.

Chapter 13

How to Win Souls for the Master

Every believer has been called to the ministry of reconciliation, the ministry of reuniting men with God just as our Lord Jesus Christ did when on earth. [2 Cor. 5: 18-20] Evangelism is the act of taking the gospel of Jesus Christ to the world. Though the word evangelist is used directly in two instances in scripture, the word evangelism does not occur in scripture, but is implied in many passages. The Greek word translated evangelism is "*euaggellos*" which can be subdivided into "*eu*" meaning good or well, and "*aggellos*" meaning message (from where the English word "angel" or "messenger" is derived). Evangelism therefore simply means good news or message. This good news is the gospel of salvation of Jesus Christ. Every Christian has been entrusted with this work, for how shall the world believe in Jesus whom they have not heard? And how shall they hear without a preacher? [Rom. 10: 14] Soul winning is the goal of evangelism. You do not evangelize to get a person to your church or to align them to your religious creed or to become a moralist. Soul winning is the act of winning lost souls or sinners into the kingdom of God from that of the devil. Every sinner is of the kingdom of the devil and as such is of him. It is called "soul winning" and not "soul getting" because you do not just walk into the kingdom of the devil, get a sinner and deposit him in the kingdom of God. The enemies are not so foolish to allow you do that. They would not just wave goodbye to one of their slaves, then fold their arms, and watch you depopulate their kingdom and populate the kingdom of your master. The enemy could do with "negotiating" the healing or deliverance of a man with you, but he will never "negotiate" the salvation of any man because he will be working against his main objective of sending men to hell. So then how do you get lost souls for your master's kingdom? You win them.

To set a prisoner free, you must first overcome the enemy that holds him captive. This clears your path to capture the sinner and bring him into your master's kingdom. To win a thing, you have to fight for it, and gratefully God our Father has made ample provision for our victory. *He has provided us with an armour complete for victory and we are instructed to adorn them fully so that we will be able to hold our ground in battle, and after all, be victorious,* **Eph. 6: 13** *for our weapons used in battle are not made by any human flesh but are made mighty through God Almighty.* **2 Cor. 10: 4**

If we do not carry out this ministry as ambassadors of Jesus Christ here on earth, we will be held responsible for whatever happens to these blind and helpless sinners and their blood will be on our heads. **Ezek. 3: 17- 21** But if we do take this gospel to them by the Holy Spirit, we would absolve ourselves of any blame for whatever happens to them if they reject the message of Christ, because this message when heard by any sinner under the conviction of the Holy Spirit will either save or condemn him, depending on what decision he eventually takes. If he accepts the message and receives Jesus into his life, he will be saved; but if he under this conviction rejects such message and decides to remain in the camp of the enemy, then he would have destroyed himself. **Mrk. 16: 16**

The great commission
(Matt. 28:18- 20; Mrk. 16: 15, 16; Acts 1: 8)

The great commission is a commandment given by the Lord Jesus to ALL believers to take this gospel of salvation to every part of the world. Scriptures let us know that whoever calls on the Name of the Lord Jesus shall be saved, but that such people cannot call upon the Name of Jesus if they have not believed in Him, and they cannot believe in Him if they have not heard this gospel, for faith comes by hearing the word of God. Similarly, they cannot hear this word if no one preaches this gospel to them. This is where believers come in. We believers in turn cannot preach to them except we are sent. **Rom. 10: 13- 17** This is where the great commission comes in. Every believer has been sent because every believer has been given the great commission. It is not for the clergy or those with the ministry of an evangelist alone as many teach, but it is for all believers. It never ended with the disciples as some teach also, but extended to everyone that believed and would believe in Jesus. Everyone who is born again has been born into this great commission. Facets of this great commission include:

1. "Go" (Matt. 28: 19) – A command to ALL believers, not just pastors or evangelists.

2. "Into all the world" (Mrk. 16: 15) – No limitation of boundary; not just one region or continent or city but in everywhere you enter.

3. "Teach all nations" (Matt. 28: 19) – Make disciples or followers of Jesus Christ in every nation; no national boundaries.

4. "Preach the gospel to every creature" (Mrk. 16: 15) – No racial or ethnic or class discrimination. Every one needs to be saved just as everyone has sinned regardless of their race or class status.

5. "Baptizing them in the Name of the Father, and of the Son, and of the Holy Spirit" (Matt. 28: 19) – "In the name of" implies "by the authority of".

6. "Teaching them to observe all things whatsoever I have commanded you" (Matt. 28: 20) – Instructing them in the way of Christ Jesus.

7. "Behold, I am with you always, even unto the end of the world" (Matt. 28: 20) – A comforting statement from Jesus, showing that He is with every believer as they carry out this great commission to confirm His word and promises in and through them. He was always present with His disciples and through His Holy Spirit He confirmed His word with signs and wonders as they carried out this commission. The "end of the world" means "end of the *aion*" or this dispensation (or age) as the Greek translation renders. Now briefly, in the program of God for man there are a total of 7 dispensations:

   ❖ Dispensation of Innocence – This lasted from the period of the creation of Adam to his fall. Here man had no knowledge of good and evil and was judged by his obedience to God's single command for him not to eat of the tree of the knowledge of good and evil, for which he failed.

   ❖ Dispensation of Conscience – This lasted from the fall of Man to the period of Noah. Having now knowledge of good and evil, the actions of man were now judged by his conscience;

in doing the right and rejecting the wrong based on his conscience. Man also failed in this respect.

❖ Dispensation of Human Government – This spanned from the time of Noah's flood to the period of Abraham. Man was judged based on his obedience to ordained laws of human government given by God, in punishing misdeeds and exalting and worshipping God. Man as well failed in this.

❖ Dispensation of Promise – This lasted from Abraham to the time of Moses. Judgment and dealings of God with man was based on the promises and covenant made the patriarchs (Abraham, Isaac, Jacob, and his sons) and with Israel. They failed several times in this too.

❖ Dispensation of the Law – This lasted from the time of Moses to the time of Jesus Christ. Man was judged by his obedience to the Law of Moses which was given by God. Man likewise failed in this.

❖ Dispensation of Grace – This is the present dispensation which the Lord Jesus implied in Matthew 28: 20. It began from the death and resurrection of Jesus Christ and will end at His second coming to earth. Judgment of man is now based on his acceptance by faith, or refusal by unbelief, of this grace which has been given to this age by Christ Jesus. Whoever rejects it is condemned to hell, whoever accepts it by faith is saved. No man is saved by observing the laws of Moses, because for whosoever keeps the laws Christ will profit him nothing. Gal. 5: 2; Eph. 2: 8, 9 The dispensation of grace marked the end of the dispensation of the law, for Christ is the end of the law for righteousness to everyone that believes Rom. 10: 4 There is no condemnation to those under this grace because the principle of this grace is life while that of works (Law of Moses) is sin and death. Rom. 8: 1, 2

❖ Dispensation of the Millennium or Divine Government – This is the period of theocracy or divine rule lasting 1,000 years beginning from the second advent of Christ. Judgment will be based on obedience to Christ Jesus and resurrected saints who would reign on earth.

Evangelism could be personal – when you share this gospel to one person at a time with the aim of winning him to Christ, or evangelism could be mass – when you share this gospel to many people simultaneously, as in a mass crusade. The subject of soul winning is one that requires a book on its own and so it cannot be fully exhausted here. I have discussed it in depth in my book "I am a soul winner!"

Now consider the following facts:

- ❖ Only about 10 percent of sinners go to church. The majority (over 90 percent) do not go to church.

- ❖ For every soul won by the church, over 30 more souls are born into non-Christian homes.

- ❖ At present, the world's population stands at about 6.36 billion people. Of these only about 33 percent are Christians, making about 67 percent (or 4.26 billion) unbelievers. Of the 33 percent who are Christians, only a small fraction are true believers. The rest are only either religious, serving a particular creed, observing regular rituals, belonging to a particular sect and/ or such like there. However let us blindly ignore this fact and focus on the 67 percent (4.26 billion people) who are not Christians. Assuming each of them live up to 70 years, which is very unlikely in this age of increased violence, health- related problems, unhealthy lifestyle and other unwholesome practices, it would mean that 61 million persons enter hell every year; 167,000 persons every day; 6,947 persons every hour; 116 persons every minute, and 2 persons every second! Do not forget that these numbers exclude many of the 33 percent of Christians who are not truly born again. We can now understand that time is of great essence if this staggering number of sinners entering hell is to be nipped in the bud. They are like sheep without shepherd, and blind men wandering on a high way.

It is quite heartrending to think that many worldly activities like some show businesses which send men to hell have penetrated many areas where the gospel has not reached. Heartrending, because many believers have fantastic opportunities to reach out to such places and the world at large for Christ but do not do it. They either wait for a Sunday service or leave it to the clergy. The sinners need us to be saved. God did not commit this gospel of salvation to the angels or any other creature, but to us. [2 Cor. 5: 18- 20] In actual fact they learn new things about the works and nature of God by observing what we do and how we live! And so if we do not share this gospel, no one would. No other creature is qualified to do this in the entire universe. The fate of sinners lies in our sharing this gospel of salvation with them. The big business firms in this world are always very vigilant, and they grab every minute opportunity to get customers to patronize them, not minding the cost. They take advantage of the television, newspapers, hand and show bills, cinemas, radio, and every means of reaching people, including person to person contact and establishing their presence in the remotest of places. If such aggressive "business evangelism" is usually effective in its objective for such people, then why not the true gospel of salvation! Advancement in technology did not occur by accident. They are infact here to minister to believers in spreading this gospel to every part of the earth!

The time is very short. This is an emergency period for every sinner. Soul winning must be handled like an emergency case in the accident and emergency unit of a proficient hospital- if the patient is not quickly attended to, you lose him. Time is very imperative and we do not have much of it.

Furthermore, in many churches soul winning is restricted to Sunday services. If we must win souls we must go outside the church where majority of them (over 90 percent) are. We should not cluster ourselves within the church and wait for Sunday services to do the soul winning. If we do this, considering the number of persons dying everyday, we can then only imagine the number of sinners that would have been fed to hell before the next church service. Even more, with only about 10 percent of such sinners coming to church, over 90 percent are likely to perish in hell. Effective evangelism (evangelism that leads to soul winning) is carried out where the sinners are – outside the church. In fact from the real meaning of the word, church services are not for sinners but for believers. It is an occasion designed for **believers** to gather and fellowship together. It is in its technical sense not meant for sinners, because a sinner is not part of the body of Christ. The Greek word for church in scripture is "*ekklesia*". It means "the called out". It denotes those who are separated (called out) from a larger group or area in order to devote themselves to a particular purpose or person, who in this case is God. Scripture tells us that every believer has been called out of the world (of which sinners belong) to serve Jesus, that they are a

*"CHOSEN generation,…a people belonging to God, (to the end) that you may show forth the praises (Grk. "**arete**" – "excellences/ virtues") of Him (God) who has called you OUT OF the darkness (world) INTO His marvelous light (salvation)"* 1 Pet. 2: 9 (KJV)

The Greek rendering of the word show forth is "***exangellos***", meaning to "widely preach or proclaim a message" ("***ex***" – "out" and "***angellos***" – "message"). It is a similar Greek rendering for evangelism. The reason why a sinner is permitted in church is because doing this wisely increases the opportunity of getting him saved when compared with shutting the doors against him, which stifles the opportunity of winning a soul for Jesus. The church should however not wrongly turn church services into the main soul winning ground where they engage in the not too fruitful "waiting game" for sinners while many of such sinners who never play to the game end up in hell.

A believer should not pass the sole responsibility of soul winning to the clergy. The clergy make up only a small percentage of believers. The greater percentage of believers is made up by the congregation. So it is the work of every believer, BOTH clergy and congregation, to seek out the lost where they are rather than wait for them to come to them. Jesus told parables of the lost coin, the lost sheep and the prodigal son. Luk. 15: 3- 32 Notice that when the coin and sheep were lost, it was the responsibility of the owner to GO OUT, search them out and bring them back. However when the prodigal son was lost, he had to find his way back to his family. He was capable of logical reasoning unlike the coin and sheep which do not have such ability to find their way back. They represent sinners while the prodigal son represents the backslidden believer. Because lost sinners cannot find their way back to God by themselves, we have to go out and search for them and bring them back to God. This is what our ministry of reconciliation is all about. Waiting for them to come to us would be very futile. Each second that ticks by hauls more of them helplessly to hell. Believers must go where the action is – outside the church. Every believer must be a soul winner.

Why Urgency in Soul Winning?

Many more sinners are entering hell than are being saved. Our Lord Jesus made a revealing statement,

"The harvest truly is plentiful, but the labourers are few" Matt. 9: 37

There are a great number of sinners who are very desperate and hungry for salvation, but they do not know how to go about it and whom to trust. And so they frustratingly struggle in sin, so unsure of their fate. They betray confidence on the outside but fear and uncertainty rules them on the inside. They are so afraid of dying in their sins and yearn to know the light of salvation. They are our harvest and we must reach out to them and harvest them. Why is this important? What happens to crops which are not harvested at the right time? They waste away! Now is the right time. The harvest is NOT about to come; it is already here in full swing and waiting for the harvesters, the soul winners. Who else could have given this information than our Lord Jesus Himself, the One who is the First and the Last? [Rev. 1: 8] Therefore there is great urgency in this regard. IF WE DO NOT REACH OUT TO THEM NOW, THEY WILL PERISH IN THEIR SINS. We never know if we would have such an opportunity again to win them for Jesus. We should also bear in mind that if they die in their sins they would be lost for ETERNITY! This certainly does not call for a "soul gamble" but for a "soul harvest"! To further buttress this point on urgency, the time left for sinners to receive the free gift of salvation is very short. Like in a soccer match, the regulation time is already up. We are in added time, at the mercy of the referee, and he is about to blow his final whistle! We should hold this motto: "If a sinner would not come to us, then we must go out to them. One thing is for sure – we must both contact each other."

Soul Winning in Scripture

Numerous biblical examples of soul winning abound in scripture. Among these include:

1. **Jesus Christ (Jhn. 4: 7- 42).** What better person to lead the way in soul winning than the Lord Himself. Jesus had visited the city of Samaria with His disciples and while His disciples were gone away to buy meat, He met with a woman at a well. From tactfully asking her for a drink, this ultimately led to His declaration of being the Christ or Saviour. [v. 26] The woman after the discussion went her way into the city declared this good news to her people and this prompted them to go and see this Jesus. What followed was a remarkable two days soul winning activity. It is recorded that many Samaritans in the

city believed in Him because of the testimony of the woman. v. 39 In the succeeding days of His stay in that city, MANY MORE believed in Him because of His own testimony. v. 41 What a harvest of souls that would have been. What started as a personal evangelism with the woman turned into a mass evangelism with many receiving eternal life, for anyone that believes in Jesus has eternal life. Jhn. 3: 15, 36

2. **Apostle Peter (Acts 2: 40, 41).** This apostle had 49 days earlier denied his master but was now totally transformed. Jesus had promised His disciples that they would receive power after the Holy Spirit came upon them, and then they would be His witnesses in all the earth. Acts 1: 8 This package of power included the ability to witness for Jesus. After receiving it, this same Peter in a mass evangelism was able to win three thousand souls for Jesus that same day. He was also instrumental in the salvation of Cornelius and his entire household. Acts 10

3. **Apostle Paul (Acts 19: 10).** The Christian walk of this apostle was that of a missionary. His life and labour was devoted to winning souls for God's kingdom, but one of note was his missionary journey to the city of Ephesus in the region of Asia. His evangelistic work in this city spanned three years, but within two years of his stay, the whole region of Asia (not just the city of Ephesus) heard the word of the Lord Jesus Christ, BOTH Jews and Greeks! There were no telephones, cars, televisions, radios, internet services or any of such modern communication tools as we have today. The region of Asia comprised the present day continent of Asia and some parts of Europe. Many believed in the Lord Jesus, renounced their evil deeds, and repented. In the city of Ephesus, the word of God grew so mightily and prevailed. v. 18- 20

4. **The early church (Acts 8: 1- 4).** The early church had become so clustered together in Jerusalem that they were not fulfilling the great commission of Jesus in taking the gospel of salvation to the uttermost parts of the earth. One of the rewards of the persecution that arose against the early church was a drastic spread of this gospel to cities beyond Jerusalem, and thus it reached out to more lost souls in need of salvation. The church was scattered abroad and their evangelism became more

effective as majority of the lost souls were outside Jerusalem. The city of Jerusalem itself had already received much of this gospel, and so why should it have received more when other cities in the earth had not even heard it in any way?

5. **Philip the Evangelist (Acts 8: 5- 12; 8: 25- 40).** Philip was one of the seven deacons, of honest report, full of the Holy Spirit and of wisdom, that was ordained by the apostles to attend to the needs of the Christians in the early church in Jerusalem. ^{Acts 6: 5} His evangelistic ministry was one of the rewards of the persecution of the early church in Jerusalem. His ministry in the city of Samaria witnessed many souls turn to Jesus Christ, with a great manifestation of the Holy Spirit. There was great joy in that city because of the salvation they had received and the miracles the Holy Spirit performed through Philip. This salvation in the entire city of Samaria was achieved because such early Christians, by the aid of the persecution, went out to where the sinners were rather than wait for the sinners to come to Jerusalem (see v. 25 of Acts 8). Receiving instruction from an angel of the Lord, Philip went down into the town of Gaza from Samaria, a distance of about 100 miles (180 km) in complete obedience. When he arrived there, under the direction of the Holy Spirit, he met an Ethiopian eunuch whose soul was really thirsty for the salvation of Jesus. He was the Minister of finance under Candace, queen of Ethiopia. His hunger for God was attested to by the fact that he left his own country Ethiopia and went into Jerusalem to worship God (a distance of over 600 miles or 960 km), and even more, he read scripture with an zeal to understand it. ^{v. 27, 30} Philip expounded the scripture verse he strove hard to comprehend at this time, and this led to his preaching the gospel of salvation unto the Ethiopian. The Ethiopian got saved with the very wonderful statement

"I believe that Jesus Christ is the Son of God" ^{v. 37}

He was baptized and was filled with the joy of Jesus Christ. ^{v. 39} Every condemnation had been lifted off his neck. Philip, after being taken away from the Ethiopian by the Spirit of God, preached the gospel of salvation in all the cities near the region of Azotus till he came to Caesarea. ^{v. 40}

Even The Women Too

Soul winning was not and is not restricted to the men folks. It is not a man's business. Does salvation apply to only men? Certainly not! Then soul winning certainly does not apply to only men too. The very first evangelist (messenger of the good news of Christ) after the resurrection of Jesus Christ was Mary Magdalene, a woman. [Jhn. 20: 18] We have seen that of the Samaritan woman, who by testifying of Jesus, led many Samaritans to Christ Jesus. [Jhn. 4: 39] The other women who followed Jesus in His earthly ministry – Mary His mother, Mary (the mother of James, Simon *Zelotes,* and Joses), Joanna the wife of Chuza (a steward of Herod), and other women that had been with Him [Luk. 24: 9- 11] – also preached the good news of the resurrection of Jesus to the disciples and were part of the great commission and the baptism in the Holy Spirit at Pentecost. [Acts 1: 14] Soul winning is a privilege that only the men should not enjoy, for he that wins souls is wise, [Prov. 11: 30] and they that are wise shall shine as the brightness of the heavens and they that turn many to righteousness shall shine as the stars forever and ever. [Dan. 12: 3] Women deserve these too.

Requirements For Soul Winning

1. **Saved.** This is the most important requirement of every soul winner. Every soul winner must be saved. An unsaved man is a blind man and his going out to win souls for Jesus is like a blind man trying to lead another blind man in the right path, which is futile. More so, every work sinner renders God is not acceptable before God; they are rather morally detestable (abominable) in His sight. [Prov. 15: 8] To render a work that is acceptable in His sight, you must first be acceptable in His sight. If anyone comes before the presence of a king with a gift, such an individual must first be accepted by the king before the gift will be accepted. How can such an unsaved person tell the world of someone he has never met personally?

2. **Surrender.** To effectively evangelize for Christ, you must surrender everything you are and everything you have to God. These include your thoughts, will, emotions, time, money, status in society and your entire being- spirit, soul, and body. Being used of God as a vessel for soul winning requires you surrendering or yielding everything to Him. And of course

why not! He is your Lord or master. Many call Him wonderful names such as "My dear Lord", "my sweet Lord", "master Jesus", "mighty Lord" and so on but have not truly understood what it means to call Him Lord. The Greek word translated Lord in scripture is "*kuriotes*" and the Hebrew word is "*adonai*". Both denote "master and owner", "the one to whom I owe my loyalty and everything". The idea behind this is that every believer having been bought by the blood of Jesus becomes His servant and He, their master. Whatever they own now belongs to Him, even their very self. They cannot do anything without His authorization. In fact according to Jewish customs, any son born to such servant inexorably belongs to the master. They execute their master's instructions, even at their own inconvenience. The long and short of it all – He was their owner in every meaning of the word. To be a soul winner, you must surrender all. The price for God's power upon your life for soul winning will cost you EVERYTHING; and you must place them at His altar of sacrifice. There are no negotiations. You either give Him all and have Him work powerfully in and through you for soul winning, or you hold back some part of you and struggle in His work.

3. **Obedient.** A soul winner must be obedient. He must listen to and follow the direction of God and not his own will. Many at times God may require us to do certain things that are not so convenient to us, or that may sound really ridiculous, but we must totally trust Him and do exactly what He wants us to do, no matter how much it cost us. Eventually we will find out how much good He meant and will be very fulfilled obeying His leading. Philip the Evangelist and deacon was instructed by God while in the city of Samaria to go to Gaza, a distance of about 100 miles (180 km) and he never knew why he was being sent by God through such a distance into that city. He just obeyed and went down there. When he got there, he found a treasured soul waiting to be harvested in the Ethiopian Minister of finance. This man was won for Jesus Christ, [Acts 8: 26- 39] and through him the gospel of salvation would in turn have spread into the whole of Ethiopia with many more Ethiopians being won for Christ. What if Philip had not obeyed? The Ethiopian Minister of finance would

not have heard the gospel, and the nation of Ethiopia in turn would not have heard this gospel at that time. So through obedience in a seemingly inconvenient situation, a man was saved and a whole nation heard the gospel of Christ. God sent Philip through such an incredible distance just for the sake of one unsaved soul. This demonstrates how valuable even one soul is to Him. Through that ostensibly unimportant one soul, a whole nation or city could hear the gospel, and our obedience to God's instruction might just make the difference! Every soul winner must therefore be obedient.

4. **Understanding (Indulgence) and Patience.** Every soul winner must exhibit patience and understanding, especially in preaching this gospel of salvation to the sinner. Many at times, a sinner may show some form of resistance to the gospel or speciously argue some truths about this gospel. Do not argue back or shout "heresy!" and in exasperation walk away; just listen to him patiently. Remember his soul is your most important priority, so avoid going into anything that would make you lose him. Even if what he says or argue is wrong, you can put him in the right perspective gently and in love after listening to him. As a medical student in university, I learnt the importance of patience and understanding in soul winning. I would visit the hospital frequently to share this gospel and pray for the sick, usually after lectures, while on call breaks and on weekends with some of my brethren in church. On several instances I encountered sinners wrongly trying to prove why they were born again and trying to attach a worldly and logical reason to their argument, even when they had not received Jesus into their lives as their Saviour. With much physical exhaustion from clinical activities intensified by a feeling that the conversation was going no where, there were times I felt I should just give myself a break. But then I was reminded of the fact that the soul is much more important than anything else, and so patience and persistence paid off with the eventual salvation of that soul. Remember it is called SOUL WINNING, and so you must persist to win the soul. Let the sinner say all he has to say while you listen patiently. With this you may tell his pattern of reasoning or any specific problem that tend to keep him attached to sin, and then

know how to approach him with your message of salvation, reveal the faults in his arguments to him in love and based on scriptures, and then lead him to Christ. I have encountered numerous situations during evangelism when people inform me they are born again and are ready to defend it till their last breath. But then I ask them the very simple question: "How do you know that you are born again?" The responses they give instantly tell you whether they are or not. The reply I get from most of them are based on personal works – I do not steal, I pray everyday, I attend fellowships and church services regularly, I pay tithes, I do not indulge in so and so sins, and such like there. The answers are mostly "I do this" or "I do not do that". After listening patiently to them, I then properly explain what it means to be born again and why their reasons do not make them born again with scriptural references. Many realize this, and I then lead them to true salvation in Jesus Christ. Every soul winner must be patient and understanding. Patience is a fruit of the Holy Spirit which every believer should manifest.

5. **Compassion (Empathy) and Love.** It is compassion that drives a believer to seek out the lost soul and bring them to Jesus Christ. NO BELIEVER can be a soul winner without compassion. It was compassion that drove Jesus while on earth to make the lives of men better. It was compassion that drove Him to the cross. It was compassion that moved Him to act. It is compassion that makes a believer win lost souls at any cost. In summary, compassion always has an element of ACTION to it. It does not just stop at sympathy or condolences but transcends far beyond that into action! This compassion comes only when we understand the plan of salvation, the consequences of a sinner dying in his sins, how blind and helpless sinners are, and their dire need for salvation, knowing that a sinner dying in his sins is a very ridiculous failure on his part as the way to salvation is already unreservedly and plainly opened to him at no cost, Jesus having already paid the price for it. It is like a student failing an examination when the answers to the questions asked are boldly displayed on his question paper. As an undergraduate, I was strongly driven by empathy in praying for the sick and

lost souls. I would enter the hospital and see patients die so helplessly, some with many tears in their eyes, so afraid of death and uncertain about their fate beyond life on earth. The relatives became so inconsolable. Some of such patients were the only children of indigent parents, around whom their world centered and many gave all they had to see their children completely healed, and would cry their hearts out like babies when all hope seemed lost. Who else could give this but Christ working in and through us. It was such compassion stirred in me that caused me to act – to share this gospel of new hope, of help, direction and comfort all implanted in the package of salvation; to pray and intercede for the sick and win souls at any cost. It was such compassion that drove me to pay the price to have souls for the kingdom of God.

God is full of compassion. [Exod. 34: 6] It was compassion that propelled Him to deliver Israel out of bondage in Egypt. It was His compassion on the human race that caused Him to leave all His glory and majesty in heaven and take the lowly form of humans. Compassion causes you to identify with the sufferings and needs of people, and not just stand afar off in mere pity. A Greek translation for compassion in scripture is "*splangchnizomai*" meaning "to have the bowels yearning". The bowels (or splangchnon) – the small intestines, liver, heart, lungs – were regarded as the seat of the emotions or feelings. And so this scriptural definition simply means "to have your emotions yearning or crying out for something". "Bowels" when used in scripture usually connotes "compassion" (For example, Matthew 14: 14). Another Greek translation for compassion – "*sumpatheo*" – means "to suffer with". [Heb. 10: 34] The Hebrew translation – "*racham*" – conveys the same meaning as "*splangchnizomai*". All these scriptural definitions point to one fact – compassion entails an emotion or feeling compelling one to act, and this is a necessary ingredient for every soul winner.

6. **Wisdom.** Every soul winner requires wisdom, especially on how to approach a sinner. Scriptures say wisdom is the principal thing and it instructs us to get it. [Prov. 4: 7] Wisdom is also needed in presenting the gospel of salvation to a sinner. It is the ability

to utilize the best possible means in achieving a desired result. In as much as salvation is indispensable, the manner in which we approach a sinner and the way we present the message of salvation can make a whole lot of difference. Our Lord Jesus utilized wisdom in winning over the Samaritan woman which further led to a great harvest of souls. [Jhn. 4: 6- 42] He also won over the Apostle Nathanael by wisdom. [Jhn. 1: 44- 51] The devil himself also utilized wisdom in deceitfully winning over Eve and her husband Adam. [Gen. 3: 1- 6] The poor wise man of Ecclesiastes 9: 13- 15 delivered his city from the siege of a great king by wisdom. This wisdom for soul winning is obtained form God and God freely calls on all who lack it to ask. [Jam. 1: 5] The wisdom from God can be obtained by:

❖ Diligent study of His word [2 Tim. 3: 15]

❖ Simply asking it of Him in faith [Jam. 1: 5; 1 Kgs. 3: 4- 12]

❖ The gift of the word of wisdom [1 Cor. 12: 7, 8; Acts 6: 9, 10]

To those sincerely working for His kingdom, God will not hesitate to furnish them with supplies to carry on the work.

7. **Interested.** Every soul winner should show interest in what a sinner says. Do not monopolize the conversation or act apathetic to what they say. This can hinder a rapport already started between both of you. Show concern. If making them be the boss of the conversation would end up winning them for Jesus, then do it. Make the sacrifice to see a soul decide for Jesus. The Apostle Paul had to adapt and carry himself along with the culture of the city he entered so as to win them over for Jesus. [1 Cor. 9: 19- 23] If he had entered a Jewish city to preach the gospel and he acted as a gentile, no Jew would probably have accepted him, needless to say listen to the gospel he preached. In the same way, if he had entered a gentile city and acted as a Jew, the gentile would probably not have received him and so, he would have lost precious souls to hell. But he had to make the sacrifice of acting as a Jew to the Jews, and a gentile to the gentiles, so that by all means he would win some for Jesus.

8. **Instruct.** A soul winner should be able to instruct new converts on how to live as a Christian. It is not just enough to leave

them as new converts since they are susceptible to falling back to their old sinful life. They therefore need to be built up to a level where they can stand on their own. This is called follow up. Such instruction should be in the following areas:

❖ Daily and personal study of the bible, especially the New Testament.

❖ Praying daily in faith.

❖ Sharing this gospel of salvation with others.

❖ Christian fellowship – finding the right church to regularly fellowship in.

Personally encourage them in their Christian walk.

9. **Intercession.** A soul winner should be an intercessor. They should be prayerful. To intercede means to plead the case of someone else before God. An intercessor is not the same as a prayer warrior. An intercessor pleads a case with God until he gets a result while a prayer warrior may just pray for a case without persisting with God to obtain a result. An intercessor is like a modern day advocate in a law court who stands before a judge (God) and pleads a case for his client (plaintiff or defendant). He does not just abandon the case half way but pursues it to a logical conclusion for his client no matter how long it lasts. Abraham, when interceding for his nephew Lot before God, persistently pleaded with God for the life of his nephew until he got the assurance from God that if He found ten righteous men in the city of Sodom, He would not destroy it (ref. Gen. 18: 20- 33). He did not just stop at fifty or forty- five or thirty righteous men, but persisted in his prayer (plea) with God until he got Him to agree for ten righteous men. If Abraham had persisted and pleaded further for at least two righteous men to be found in the city for it to be spared God's wrath, God would have probably granted it to him. He however thought for sure that at least ten righteous men would be found in a city as large as Sodom. But he was wrong; there were only four righteous persons in that city. In the same way, a soul winner should be able to intercede for both lost souls and new converts; lost souls – that the Spirit of God may convict them and draw them to salvation in Jesus

Christ; new converts – that they may grow up spiritually in Christ Jesus, remain steadfast in their new faith, and in the end to never be found wanting in the kingdom of God. Prayers also need to be made for soul winners who are the harvesters of the crops of lost souls. Jesus Christ instructed us to pray (petition; plead with) that God send forth more labourers (soul winners) into His harvest because the harvest itself (souls waiting to be won for the kingdom of God) is abundant but the labourers are lacking. [Matt. 9: 37, 38] The Greek word translated "send forth" in verse 38 is "*ekballo*" meaning "to thrust out or forcefully eject something". This depicts the urgency attached to harvesting lost souls for the kingdom, hence the petitions required for God to forcefully send out the soul winners to where they ought to be – out in the field harvesting lost souls for the kingdom of God.

10. **No Procrastination.** Soul winning is a "NOW" thing and not a "later" or future thing. Consider the fact that about 2 persons enter hell every second, and that time given to sinners to receive salvation through Jesus is almost up, then we will understand why procrastination is a great enemy of the soul winner. Never post pone soul winning to the future when you can do it right now! You can never tell how many souls you would win for Christ within the period you delay, and more importantly, you will never be able to tell if you would have such an opportunity again.

11. **Respectful or Humble.** As a soul winner do not keep yourself aloof from sinners or interact with them from a distance in the figurative sense. This "Pharisee approach" only ends up creating a divide in communication between you and the sinner which hardly results in soul winning. Jesus was able to win sinners to be His disciples because He never kept a distance from them. Never act in a way that shows the sinner that he is far too inferior to you, or that interacting with him will "stain your holy garments." Consider our Lord Jesus. How was He able to win a man as wealthy as Matthew to be His disciple? Matthew was a tax collector, a multimillionaire by modern reckoning. When called by Jesus he left his very lucrative job and became a disciple. [Matt. 9: 9] Or how about

Zacchaeus who was not just a tax collector, but a chief one, [Luk. 19: 2] or the Apostles Peter, James and John who had a thriving fishing business empire? At least scripture lets us know that the family of James and John (the Zebedee family) had a boat and hired servants. [Mrk. 1: 19, 20] To win lost souls, we must lower ourselves to them rather than maintain the distance.

12. **Reliance.** The soul winner must rely on two factors for direction – the word of God and the Holy Spirit. These two are the guiding light of any believer on earth. A believer must know and understand the word of God through study, especially the plan of salvation as this is important in presenting the gospel to a sinner in a very simple way. You must also develop a relationship with the Holy Spirit. The Holy Spirit is the one who convicts the sinner, He is the one who empowers you to do exploits for Jesus as a soul winner, He is the one who stirs you up for the work of God, He makes the work of soul winning exhilarating, and He is the one that qualifies you for the work. Not all work for God is acceptable in His sight; only that which is done by the Holy Spirit is acceptable before God. He is the one that opens up your understanding to the word of God. Every work of soul winning recorded in scripture was enabled by Him. The book of Acts is actually the Acts of the Holy Spirit through the disciples. He is an indispensable personality in the life of every believer.

The secret of getting Him to act through you is to know Him personally and this comes by spending much time with Him in prayer and bible study. I like to describe it as enrolling in the University of the Holy Spirit where learning never ends but gets deeper with each higher level attained. God the Father is the Chancellor, God the Son is the Vice Chancellor, and the Holy Spirit is the sole Professor and lecturer, and every believer is a student. If you do not attend lectures or do the assignments given to you by the Holy Spirit, how then can He graduate you and confer with Ph.D. honours, which is the power of God? The more time you spend with the Holy Spirit in His lecture classroom, the more you will know Him and rely on Him. Moses had spent forty days on Mount Horeb with God, and when he came down from the mountain to the people, they saw the glory of the Lord radiating from his face like horns and were afraid to look at him. And even more, Moses <u>never knew</u> that the glory of the Lord on him was that immense to have been outwardly manifested! Dear friend, he never asked God for it. It was simply a natural product of much time spent with God. ^{Exod. 34: 28- 30} In another instance, when the rulers, elders and scribes in Jerusalem saw the boldness with which Apostles Peter and John spoke, the miracles wrought by God through them, and that they were illiterates, they marveled at what was done. They did not ask any questions but instantly knew that these men HAD BEEN WITH JESUS. ^{Acts 4: 13} The works of the disciples was also a result of much time spent as students in the spiritual University of the Holy Spirit during the time of Jesus. They may have been worldly illiterates but they were spiritual intellects. Every great man or woman of God that ever walked on the surface of this earth passed through this university and were bestowed with honours by none other than the Lord Jesus Himself. What else can you expect from a student who studies at the best university and under the best ever known Professor? You certainly would not expect anything less than what they did!

13. **Responsibility.** The soul of every sinner is the responsibility of every believer. We are the only ones in the entire universe – heaven, earth, beneath the earth – that have this gospel of salvation and we are the only ones that can preach this gospel. In the region of Caesarea was a man called Cornelius. He was a devout man but was not saved. God had to send His angel to instruct Cornelius to send for Peter who would lead him and his household to salvation in Christ. ^{Acts 10} Now why did God not send His angel to preach this gospel to Cornelius rather than send for Peter to do the job? That is because only a believer could do the job! The principalities and powers learn about God's saving works through believers. ^{Eph. 3: 10} Even the angels in heaven who intensely desire to know these things ^{1 Pet. 1: 12} gaze at the believers in wonder as they carry out the wonderful work of soul winning. They are spectators, and not participants in this ministry. The salvation of the lost souls depends on our preaching this gospel. The Holy Spirit needs us in order to convict them. Failure to cooperate and carry

out our duty will place the blood of the sinner if he dies in his sins upon our heads. [Ezek. 33: 8] We have been made watchmen unto the world to sound the trumpet of God's judgments upon sinners, and to proclaim the salvation of Jesus Christ. If we do carry out this responsibility, then the onus of deciding for Christ will now rest on the shoulders of the sinner.

14. **Eagerness (Zeal).** Every believer must be zealous for lost souls. Zeal drives the believer to the lost souls, wisdom gets the results.

All these requirements can be recalled with the acronym: S^{2}OUL WI^{2}NE^{2}R^3

S – Saved; Surrender
O – Obedience
U – Understanding (Indulgence) and Patience
L – Listen (Show interest)
W – Wisdom
I – Instruct; Intercession
N – Now (No Procrastination)
E – Empathy (Compassion) and Love; Eagerness (Zeal)
R – Respectful (Humble); Responsibility; Reliance (on God's Word and the Holy Spirit).

Communicating the Gospel To The Sinner

In presenting the gospel message, the plan of salvation should be presented in a very simple and comprehensible manner. Do not turn yourself into a professor of Theology. Many sinners are really put off by such approach. Remember, they understand very little of scriptures. So be as simple as possible. Do not use too many scripture verses and do not be too technical. The manner in which you expound a scriptural fact to a believer should differ from that of a sinner who most often has no background knowledge of scripture. More so do not use that as an opportunity to show off to others that you are winning a soul for Christ or to flaunt yourself as a soul winning *"guru"* as this may be embarrassing to the sinner.

Approaching a sinner

Approaching a sinner differs depending on the existing situation. This is only to serve as a guide and so you must adapt yourself to the prevailing situation.

1. **Establish a rapport.** When you meet an individual you intend to win for Christ, moving straight to discuss salvation of the soul issues might backfire. Some are usually not interested in anything salvation and so if you initiate this topic immediately, the discussion might as well end there. The first thing you need to do is to establish a rapport by discussing what you think the person might be interested in. This may be related to sports, business, fashion, music, academics, hobbies, job or some story. This gets them interested and makes them feel so much at ease talking with you. When they realize how humble and attentive you are to them, they become humble and attentive also, and it now becomes easier to deviate the discussion in your direction. This is very much like meeting a new friend, introducing yourself and initiating a discussion.

2. Then gradually begin to **assess the level of spirituality** of the person, or how much attention he gives to spiritual matters. You can introduce this into the discussion as it proceeds. You can ask questions such as:

    ❖ Have you given thought to life after now?

    ❖ What do you think is the role of the church in so and so issue?

    ❖ So many people have different ideas about the place called heaven (or hell). What do you think?

    The answer he gives to the question will provide you an idea of how much interest he gives to spiritual matters.

3. Irrespective of the answer given in step 2, go on to the next step which delves further in the direction of salvation. You can ask the question:

    ❖ What do you think is the greatest spiritual need of an individual?

Different answers would ensue from this question. Some may say shelter, some food, some money, some love, some might humbly say they do not know, others might rightly say salvation. This does not mean they are born again. If they rightly say salvation, then move straight on to step 4. If they answer otherwise, HUMBLY point out the different view which scripture holds. The subject of salvation then comes into play. You can say:

"You are right that we all need this (mention name), but you know scripture holds a very different view. It talks about salvation of the soul as the greatest need"

Some might argue while others might humbly agree. If they argue, DO NOT argue back. Many always want to be right, especially those that feel too intellectual. If you argue with them, even if you rightly do so, you may win the argument but lose them. Remember, apply wisdom! Make them feel like the captain but "steer the ship" in your direction. You must promote an ambiance of cordiality and not tension. Do not take disagreements seriously. Laugh or smile over them! This makes them more at ease and more willing and excited to continue the discussion with you, and respond to your questions. Even if you end up not concurring on this, you would have at least succeeded in doing one thing – bringing up the issue of salvation!

4. Now that you have tactfully brought up the issue of salvation, you can then ask questions around it to **find out if they are saved**. You can ask:

❖ Have you received the salvation of Jesus?

❖ Have you given thought to the salvation of your soul?

To the first question, some might honestly tell you they have not received it. Some might require you to explain what salvation means. This shows that they are not saved. The answer they give will tell you if they are saved (born again) or not. Remember, the ultimate objective is to lead them to Jesus Christ. If they are not saved, then move on to step 6 and lead them to salvation in Jesus. Some might frankly tell you they are saved or born again. This however does not necessarily mean they are truly saved. You must understand what they mean when they say they are saved.

5. It is now up to you to **find out what they mean** when they say they are saved. You can ask the question:

    ❖ Why do you say you are saved? OR

    ❖ What do you mean when you say you are saved? OR

    ❖ How do you know that you are saved?

    Some might say they are saved because they attend church regularly, they pray and fast and study scriptures regularly, they do not lie, steal, swear, keep bad company or fornicate; they confess their sins regularly to their pastors and brethren, and all those "good works stuff". This should tell you that they are not saved. You should then HUMBLY explain what salvation means and why they are not saved by such reasons they gave. Be sure to use scriptural examples! You can say: "Please I would like to show you some scripture verses right here." Pull out your bible and use your finger to point at the particular verse you are referencing, and do not use too many verses. As much as possible use a single book of scripture for referencing.

    If they however give the right reason for being saved – believing in the finished work of Jesus for them, and receiving Him into their lives as Lord and Saviour – then you have a brother or sister in Christ Jesus!

    Remember that salvation is not by coercion. If they do not receive Jesus after this, you cannot force them. You would have played your part in sharing this gospel with them. Do not however give up on them. Persistently share this gospel with them if you have other opportunities of meeting them, until they finally decide for Christ Jesus.

6. Now **present the plan of salvation** in a very concise and simple way to them. This should include the glorious state of man before his fall, the fall of man and God's plan to redeem him; how God's love for him compelled Him to give out His only begotten Son to pay the costly price which he could not pay for his salvation; the work of Jesus on the cross and its

significance – reconciling man to God, salvation and other blessings of God. Do not leave out the consequences of his refusing this salvation – eternal condemnation in hell and subsequently the Lake of fire; emphasize more on the love of Jesus Christ for him. Let this love under the conviction of the Holy Spirit draw him to willingly surrender to Christ. Do not present hell as a THREAT, but as a WARNING. Rely totally on the Holy Spirit for direction.

Having done this, invite them to receive Jesus into their lives and be saved. Remember, they are to voluntarily make this decision. Do not impose it on them. If they yield to the conviction of the Holy Spirit, they would so gladly do this. You can say:

"(Mention name of the person), would you like to receive salvation right now?"

If he agrees, take hold of his hands, bow your head and ask him to repeat this prayer after you:

"My dear Lord Jesus". Wait for him to repeat after you. Then continue.

"I acknowledge and openly confess that I am a sinner and in need of salvation"

"Forgive me of all my sins…"

"And cleanse me of all unrighteousness"

"I believe you died for my sins and were raised from the dead"

"I receive you into my life as my personal Saviour"

"Come and make your home in me and be my master"

"I yield myself to you…"

"Work in and through me as you will"

"I believe I am saved."

"Thank you for saving me."

"In Jesus' Name. AMEN.

Do not rush through this prayer, but be sure he repeats it after you. Now that you have led him to Christ Jesus, do not leave him at this point. Make it your responsibility to ensure that he is established in Christ.

❖ Take him to church and help him integrate into it by meeting with other brethren, attending fellowships and other meetings.

❖ Help him with daily bible study and prayer. Assist him with supply of bible devotionals and literature that would edify him.

❖ Encourage him in sharing this gospel of salvation to others. Let him accompany you and other brethren, and before long, another soul winner would have been produced! A chain reaction of soul winning then begins. Imagine what happens if a person wins at least 10 souls to Christ. Each of these 10 souls wins another 10 souls, totaling 100 souls. Each of these 100 souls wins another 10 souls, making 1000 souls, and so on.

Some helpful scripture verses for these steps include:

Step 5 – Romans 10: 4; (Ephesians 2: 8)

Step 6 – Romans 10: 9, 10, 13.

**The above is only a guide on how to approach a sinner. Just as individuals and situations differ, so should your approach. Utilize wisdom and let the Holy Spirit guide you on how to approach a sinner.

Tackling Unfounded Excuses of Sinners

So many give excuses regarding why they cannot be born again. As a believer and soul winner, you should be prepared to handle them with scriptural backing. Some of these excuses include:

1. Salvation is not for everyone – Rom. 1: 16; 10: 13; Jhn. 6: 37.

2. I am afraid I cannot keep the faith – Rom. 14: 4; Heb. 7: 25; 1 Pet. 1: 5.

3. I believe everyone will be saved – Mrk. 16: 16; Gal. 5: 19- 21.

4. The Christian life is too difficult to live – Rom. 6: 23; 1 Cor. 10: 13.

5. I do not believe in hell – Matt. 10: 28; Luk. 16: 19- 31.

6. I do not believe in God – Psa. 14: 1; Rev. 21: 8; Mrk. 16: 16.

7. My friends would mock me – Matt. 5: 10- 12.

8. It is hard to become saved – Rom. 1: 16; Jhn. 1: 12.

9. I will get saved sometime later; but not now – Heb. 2: 3; 3: 15; Isai. 55: 6; Luk. 12: 20.

10. I am already religious – Matt. 18: 3; Gal. 5: 19- 21.

11. God is too good to allow me tormented in hell – Mrk. 16: 16; Jhn. 3: 16- 18; Prov. 1: 24- 33.

12. I live a morally upright life – Luk. 16: 15; Rom. 3: 10- 23; Jam. 2: 10; 1 Jhn. 3: 8- 10.

13. Everyone is a child of God – 2 Tim. 2: 19; Rom. 8: 9- 16.

14. I am too young to be saved – Matt. 18: 3; 2 Cor. 6: 2.

15. I cannot give up certain things – Rom. 8: 1- 5; 2 Cor. 5: 17- 21; Col. 3: 2; 1 Jhn. 1: 9.

16. God will save me when He wants to – Mrk. 1: 15; 2 Pet. 3: 9.

Excuses of Backsliders

1. I cannot be lost regardless of what I do – 1 Cor. 3: 17; 9: 27; Gal. 5: 19- 21.

2. God will not take me back – Gal. 4: 19; 1 Jhn. 1: 9.

3. I have committed blasphemy of the Holy Spirit (the unpardonable sin) – Heb. 6: 4- 6; 10: 26- 29.

Chapter 14

100 Living Words For Your Treasure Chest

*T*he bible is filled with inestimable and wonderful promises and blessings from God. These promises and blessings are for His children, and now that you are born again, they are yours to treasure! What could be more than that? They are God's words and you can be sure of one thing, God never fails to keep His words or promises. [Psa. 33: 9; Isai. 34: 16] He has said that He is faithful (even in His word). He has also said that when He speaks His word, it will NEVER come back to Him until it has accomplished the purpose for which He sent it. [Isai. 55: 10, 11]

In this chapter, I have prayerfully chosen 100 words in scripture that our Father, the Almighty God has spoken. This is specially for you and for you to hold onto in your spirit. These are promises, blessings, and instructions most of which are drawn from the New Testament with some applications to your life. They remind you of who you are in Christ, and the promises and blessings that you have in Him. Personalize them! They are yours!

1. You know that you are now a child of God by the Holy Spirit, and an heir of God and joint heir with Christ Jesus (Rom. 8: 15- 17).

2. You know that your sins have been washed by the blood of Jesus (Rev. 1: 5).

3. You know you have been redeemed to God by the blood of Jesus (Eph. 1: 7; Rev. 5: 9).

4. You know that you have the life of Christ Jesus in you, for God has given you eternal life and this life is in His Son (Jesus). He who has the Son has life. These things have been written to you who believe in the name of the Son of God that you may know that you have eternal life (1 Jhn. 5: 11- 13).

5. Now you are in Christ Jesus, there is no longer any condemnation against you (Rom. 8: 1); sin will no longer have control over you because you are now under the grace of Jesus (Rom. 6: 14).

6. You know that the same Jesus that saved you from eternal death is also able to keep you from falling into sin and present you blameless before the throne of God (Jude v. 24), for He who has started a good work in you will see it to completion till the coming of the Lord Jesus (Php. 1: 6).

7. You know that you live by faith (Heb. 10: 38; Rom. 1: 16) – of Jesus who loved you and gave Himself for you (Gal. 2: 20).

8. You know that by grace you are saved through faith in Jesus and not by works (Eph. 2: 8, 9), for by deeds of the law no flesh will be justified in the sight of God (Rom. 3: 20) and Christ is the end of the law for righteousness to everyone who believes (Rom. 10: 4).

9. You know that you are a king and priest in the service of God (Rev. 1: 6; 1 Pet. 2: 9).

10. You know that the Lord always watches over you, for His eyes are on the righteous (1 Pet. 3: 12).

11. You know that you are enthroned with Jesus in heaven (Eph. 2: 6), and you are complete in Him who is the head of all principality and power (Col. 2: 9).

12. You know that every situation no matter how bad it seems is only working out for your good, since God has said that ALL things work together for your good because you love God, and you are the called according to His purpose (Rom. 8: 28).

13. You know that now you have eternal life in Christ Jesus, you should continually hold on to it and never let it go (1 Tim. 6: 12).

14. You know that you should always rejoice in the Lord (Php. 4: 4), for in His presence is FULLNESS of joy (Psa. 16: 11).

15. You know that God never has evil plans or thoughts against you, but His thoughts for you are ALWAYS of peace, to give you a future and a hope (Jerem. 29: 11).

16. You know that the promises of God for you will never fail (Isai. 34: 16); for whatever promises are of God, in Christ Jesus they are confirmed for you (2 Cor. 1: 20) and God is not man that He should lie (Num. 23: 19).

17. You know that you now belong to the genealogy of Christ Jesus and so do not regard any one from the flesh (human) point of view, because you are a new creation in Christ Jesus (2 Cor. 5: 16, 17).

18. If you sin inadvertently, you know that Jesus Christ your advocate in heaven constantly intercedes for you before the Father (1 Jhn. 2: 1, 2). Moreover, if you confess your sins, He is faithful and just to forgive you your sins and to cleanse you from all unrighteousness (1 Jhn. 1: 9).

19. You know that you should now not dwell on your past flaws, because as far as the east is from the west (as far as infinity is from infinity), so has God taken your sins away from you (Psa. 103: 12), and He will NEVER remember them again, for as long as you live (Isai. 43: 25). You should therefore not dwell on them because they can hinder your fellowship with the Holy Spirit.

20. You know that you have a very dependable friend and advocate in the Holy Spirit who makes intercession for you with groanings that words cannot express (Rom. 8: 26, 27).

21. You know that you live and walk with God not by your ability but by the Holy Spirit (Zech. 4: 6), for it is not of him who wills nor of him who runs, but of God who shows mercy (Rom. 9: 16).

22. You know that God urges you to call on Him, and has promised to answer you and show you great and inaccessible things which you do not know (Jer. 33: 3).

23. You know that WHATEVER you ask of God, you receive from Him BECAUSE you keep His commandments and do those things that are pleasing in His sight; and this is His commandment – that you should believe on the name of His Son Jesus Christ and love one another (1 Jhn. 3: 22, 23).

24. You therefore know that your Father in heaven will not with hold the Holy Spirit from you if you keep asking Him (Luk. 11: 13) in faith (Jhn. 7: 37- 39).

25. You know that whatever things you ask when you pray, you should BELIEVE that you receive them and you will have them (Mrk. 11: 24), for all things are possible to him who believes (Mrk. 9: 23).

26. You know that your life here on earth is to Christ Jesus (Php. 1: 21), that you may please Him in all things (2 Tim 2: 4).

27. You know that you have been entrusted by the Lord with the ministry of reconciling sinners back to God (2 Cor. 5: 18, 19).

28. You know that you ought to give thanks to God IN EVERY SITUATION (1 Thess. 5: 18), because ALL THINGS will work together for your good (Rom. 8: 28).

29. You know that you are now the righteousness of God in Christ Jesus (2 Cor. 5: 21).

30. You know that God resists the proud and gives grace to the humble (Jam. 4: 6).

31. You also know that God dwells in a high and holy place, but also with him who has a contrite and humble spirit, to revive the spirit of the humble and to revive the heart of the contrite (Isai. 57: 15).

32. You know that you should therefore be like minded as Christ Jesus, humbling yourself before God as He did (Php. 2: 5- 8) and God in due time will exalt you (Jam. 4: 10).

33. You know that you should be persistent in prayer (Col. 4: 2) because the effective, fervent prayer of a righteous man avails much (Jam. 5: 16).

34. You know that God will NEVER leave you nor forsake you. As such you are confident that He is always with you in every

situation or challenge (Isai. 43: 2), and so you can boldly face anything (Heb. 13: 5, 6; Matt. 28: 20).

35. You know that your labour for God will never be in vain (1 Cor. 15: 58), because every labourer is worthy of his wages (Luk. 10: 7; 1 Tim. 5: 18).

36. You know that you should first seek the kingdom of God and His righteousness, and all other things will be added to you (Matt. 6: 33).

37. You know that your life is hidden with Christ in God (Col. 3: 3), and so you have no need to fear anything.

38. You know that you should speak evil of no one, but be humble to all men, and be careful to maintain good works (Tit. 3: 8).

39. You know that you should not let any corrupt word proceed out of your mouth, but what is good for necessary edification that it may impart grace to the hearers (Eph. 4: 29).

40. You know that you should set your mind on heavenly things, and not on things on the earth (Col. 3: 2), where moth and rust destroy and where thieves break in and steal (Matt. 6: 19). It will profit you nothing if you gain the whole world and lose your soul (Mrk. 8: 36).

41. You know that you should not be unequally yoked together with unbelievers (2 Cor. 6: 14), for evil communication corrupts good manners (1 Cor. 15: 33).

42. You know that you must act out your faith, for faith without works is dead just as the body without the spirit is dead (Jam. 2: 17, 26).

43. You know that you should let our requests be made known to God (Php. 4: 6), for you do not have what you desire because you do not ask (Jam. 4: 2).

44. You know that when you ask, you should ask in faith, without doubting, because a man that doubts in asking is double minded and unstable in his ways and so will not receive anything from the Lord (Jam. 1: 6- 8).

45. You know that God will not allow a temptation which is beyond you to come your way and will always make for you a way of escape from it (1 Cor. 10: 13).

46. You know that your Lord Jesus set an example for you in overcoming temptations rather than yielding to it, for He was in all points tempted as every believer is, yet He was without sin (Heb. 4: 15).

47. You know that you have the reward of the crown of life for enduring temptations and not yielding to them (Jam. 1: 12).

48. You know that because God is your shepherd, you shall not lack (Psa. 23: 1), for He shall supply all your needs according to His riches in glory by Christ Jesus (Php. 4: 19).

49. You know that you should work out your own salvation with fear and trembling (Php. 2: 12).

50. You know that you should constantly discipline your body and bring it under your control, so that you would not fall to its sinful desires and in the end become a castaway (1 Cor. 9: 27), as rejected silver (Jerem. 6: 30).

51. You know that you should diligently study scriptures in order to present yourself approved of God, a worker who does not need to be ashamed but who precisely expounds the word of truth (2 Tim. 2: 15).

52. You know that you should let the word of Christ (scriptures) richly make a home in you (Col. 3: 16).

53. You know that you should be sober at all times (Luk. 21: 36) and maintain an uninterrupted and constant spirit of prayer (1 Thess. 5: 17; Luk. 18: 1).

54. You know that as a believer, you are anointed of God, and you know all things spiritually (1 Jhn. 2: 20; 2 Cor. 1: 21).

55. You know that you owe your brethren the duty of love (Rom. 13: 8), for everyone that loves is born of God and knows God (1 Jhn. 4: 7) and has transited from death to eternal life (1 Jhn. 3: 14).

56. You know that it is the will of God that you flourish in ALL things and enjoy good health, even as your soul already prospers in Christ Jesus (3 Jhn. v.2).

57. You are confident that the Lord hears your prayers (1 Jhn. 5: 14), for His ears are open to your prayers (1 Pet. 3: 12), and because you know He hears you in whatever you ask Him, you know that you have the thing you have asked of Him (1 Jhn. 5: 15).

58. You know that you have overcome the enemy because of the blood of Jesus, and because of the word of your testimony (Rev. 12: 11).

59. You know that you should be swift to hear, not hasty to speak and not hasty to anger (Jam. 1: 19), because in the multitude of words sin is not lacking (Prov. 10: 19) and a man quickly angered acts foolishly (Prov. 14: 17). More so, the anger of man does not produce the righteousness of God (Jam. 1: 20).

60. You know that the principles of God remain the same in all the ages (dispensations), for He is unchangeable (Mal. 3: 6) and He remains the same yesterday, today and forever (Heb. 13: 8).

61. You know that God has set a principle of holiness for you, without which you cannot see Him (Heb. 12: 14).

62. You therefore know that just as God is holy you also must be holy in all your conduct (1 Pet. 1: 15, 16).

63. You know that your body is the temple of the Holy Spirit (1 Cor. 3: 16; 6: 19) and you should therefore surrender your body as an instrument of righteousness unto God (Rom. 6: 13) rather than defile the temple of God by sin.

64. You know that whoever defiles this temple will not go unpunished (1 Cor. 3: 17). You therefore know that you should not allow sin to reign in your body (Rom. 6: 12), you should flee sexual immorality and every other sin that defiles God's temple (1 Cor. 6: 18; Eph. 5: 3; 2 Tim. 2: 22).

65. You know that if you search for God diligently through prayer and worship, you will surely find Him (Jerem. 29: 13; Matt. 7: 7), for everyone that keeps seeking will find (Luk. 11: 9, 10).

66. You know that you can do all things through Christ who strengthens you (Php. 4: 13), because He has made you more

than a conqueror in all things (Rom. 8: 37) and ALWAYS leads you in triumph (2 Cor. 2: 14).

67. You know that you have not been given a spirit of fear, but of power and of love and of a sound mind (2 Tim. 1: 7).

68. You know that healing has been provided for you, because by the stripes of Jesus you have been healed (1 Pet. 2: 24).

69. You know the works of the devil (Jhn. 10: 10) and so you must be sober and vigilant because your enemy the devil walks about like a roaring lion seeking whom he may devour (1 Pet. 5: 8).

70. Therefore, you know that you should resist the devil and he will flee from you. Then draw near to God and He draw near to you (Jam. 4: 7, 8).

71. You know that you have been given ALL things that concerns life and how to worship God the right way (2 Pet. 2: 3), and God has blessed you with EVERY spiritual blessing in heaven (Eph. 1: 3).

72. You know that you are more than victorious in all things through Jesus Christ (Rom. 8: 37), because you are born of God, for whoever is born of God overcomes the world by his faith (in Jesus) (1 Jhn. 5: 4).

73. You know that love of the world means an enmity with God, for all that is in the world – the lust of the flesh, and the lust of the eyes, and the pride of life – is not of God your Father but is of the world (1 Jhn. 2 : 15, 16).

74. You do not have the nature or ability to sin because you are born of God and have His divine nature in you (1 Jhn. 3: 9).

75. You know that the gospel of Jesus is to you the power of God for the salvation of ALL that believes it (1 Cor. 1: 18; Rom. 1: 16).

76. You know that sinners cannot believe in Jesus if they do not hear this gospel, and they cannot hear this gospel if you do not let them know (Rom. 10: 14).

77. You know that you have been sent by the Lord Jesus to preach this gospel to them (Matt. 28: 19, 20).

78. You know that you ought not to walk by sight (physical senses) but by faith (2 Cor. 5: 7).

79. You know that there are no limits to what God can do for you, for He is able to do exceedingly abundantly above all that you ask or think, according to the power that works in you (Eph. 3: 20). He is the God of all flesh and nothing is too hard for Him to do (Jerem. 32: 27; Matt. 19: 26).

80. You know that you should put on the FULL armour of God that you may be able to stand against the wiles of the devil (Eph. 6: 11), for the weapons by which you wage war are not of the flesh, but are made mighty by God to pull down strongholds, demolish reasonings and every barrier that raises itself against the knowledge of God, leading into captive every thought to the obedience of Christ (2 Cor. 10: 4, 5).

81. You know that your fight is not directed to the physical (against flesh and blood) but is spiritual – against principalities, authorities, rulers of the darkness of this world, the spiritual forces of wickedness in the heavenly places (Eph. 6: 12).

82. You know that you should not be ignorant of the armour by which you wage this spiritual battle (Eph. 6: 14- 18).

83. You know that you should continually be filled with the Holy Spirit (Eph. 5: 18, 19) by constant fellowship with Him (2 Cor. 13: 14).

84. You know that you must pay the price of dying daily (1 Cor. 15: 31) to yourself and the world if you are to be a follower of Jesus and walk in His power, for if any man desires to follow Jesus, he must deny himself, and take up his cross daily and follow Him (Luk. 9: 23).

85. You know that even though no disciple is greater than his teacher, he shall be like his teacher when perfectly trained (Luk. 6: 40). You should therefore follow the examples of Jesus if you are to be like Him.

86. You know that your citizenship is in heaven (Php. 3: 20) and you have the Holy Spirit in you as a guarantee to this (2 Cor. 1: 22).

87. You know that you should not conform yourself to the things of this world, but be transformed by the renewing of your mind. Then you will be able to test and know what God's good and acceptable and perfect will is (Rom. 12: 2).

88. You know that you have been given grace that qualifies you to partake of the gifts of Jesus (Eph. 4: 7, 8). And so you should activate the gift of God in you to attain higher levels, because to him that has more will be given, but to him that does not have, that which he has shall be taken away from him (Luk. 19: 26).

89. You know that you are the light of the world and you should let this light so shine before men that they may see your good works and glorify your Father in heaven (Matt. 5: 14, 16).

90. You know that you should not grieve the Holy Spirit by engaging in evil works (Eph. 4: 30, 31).

91. You know that the throne of God is the throne of grace, and that the blood of Jesus has given you boldness to come before this throne and obtain (collect) mercy and find the grace to assist you in the time of your need (Heb. 4: 16).

92. You know that you are complete in Christ Jesus in whom all the fullness of the Godhead dwells bodily (Col. 2: 9, 10).

93. You know that God will keep you in perfect (complete) peace when you keep Him in your thoughts and trust in Him (Isai. 26: 3).

94. You know that God is the source of your sustenance, for in Him you live and move and have your being (Acts 17: 28), and the life you now live in the flesh you live by the faith of Jesus Christ, who loved you and gave Himself for you (Gal. 2: 20).

95. You know that the Holy Spirit is always with you to help you in your weaknesses (Rom. 8: 26). You know that He teaches all things (Jhn. 14: 26), guides you into all truth and reveals God in a real way to you (Jhn. 16: 13- 15).

96. You know that you should carry out this great commission (Matt. 28: 19, 20) while you still have the time, because the day comes when this will not be possible (Jhn. 9: 4).

97. You know that at the coming of the Lord Jesus Christ, your physical body will be transformed into a spiritual one, to be conformed to His own glorious body (Php. 3: 20, 21; 1 Cor. 15: 44).

98. You know that you should hold on to your faith in Christ Jesus, so that in the end when Christ Jesus calls you home to heaven, you can look back at your life on earth and say like the Apostle Paul, "I have fought the good fight (of faith), I have finished the race (set for me on earth), I have kept the faith" (2 Tim. 4: 7).

99. You know that the crown of righteousness awaits you in heaven, when you finish your race here on earth (2 Tim. 4: 8).

100. You know that you cannot afford to miss the wedding feast of Jesus in heaven! (Rev. 19: 7- 9).

Chapter 15

Scriptures for Moments Like These

*T*here are moments when your faith in God is tested, your salvation is put in doubt, the pains seem unending, the tears seem ceaseless, your needs become apparent, and it seems sickness and infirmity has laid a hold on your body. These are not times to fret. These are times to overcome with the sword of the Spirit- the very word of the living God. Moments like these call for the scriptures in your spirit being released unto your tongue for utterance. This calls for meditation of scripture. Speak this word IN FAITH to arrest that situation. Refuse to believe what you feel by your senses; rather believe what the word of God says concerning your situation. Remember, scripture is the WORD OF GOD. It is like God speaking directly to you regarding your situation. The only difference is that in scripture this spoken word of God is put down in writing. The word of God is eternal [Isai. 40: 8] and is ever living and active, [Heb. 4: 12] whether it was spoken three thousand years ago or just a week ago. It still has the same potency! It is a messenger sent by Him to people- it always achieves the purpose for which He sends it forth before it returns to Him. [Isai. 55: 10, 11] Jesus is the same yesterday, today, and forever. [Heb. 13: 8]

Now suppose you had a particular sickness in your body and Jesus suddenly appears physically to you and says to you directly, "My dear child, you are healed by My stripes". You certainly would take His word for it hook, line and sinker because of His physical presence. It is the same as when you speak His word in scripture to the sickness, even in His physical absence. You see, even though Jesus is not physically present with us believers, His presence ever remains with us by His Holy Spirit who is also called the Spirit of Christ:

*"But you are not in the flesh but in the Spirit, if so be that the Spirit of God is making His home in you. Now if any man have not the **Spirit of Christ**, he is none of His."* Rom. 8: 9

*"Searching what, or what manner of time the **Spirit of Christ** who was in them did signify when He testified beforehand the sufferings of Christ, and the glory that should follow"* 1 Pet. 1: 11

This was what Jesus meant in Matthew 28: 20 when He said,

"...and, lo, I am with you alway till the end of the age (Grk. "dispensation"). Amen."

The Holy Spirit is spirit, Jhn. 4: 24 and you cannot see or know a spirit with your physical eyes. To see (perceive) a spirit, you must see with the eyes of faith, which is your spirit. The same applies with the Holy Spirit. To perceive or know Him, you must utilize the eyes of your spirit, which are the eyes of faith. With these eyes of faith, His spiritual presence becomes as physical presence. The fact that many do not feel His presence does not mean He is not there. On the contrary, He is and will always be there. So faith ever remains indispensable to the believer in his walk with God and to receive from Him. And this faith comes by the WORD OF GOD. Rom. 10: 17 His word is spirit and life. Jhn. 6: 63 It is an evidence of His presence. All that is required of you is to ONLY BELIEVE. Mrk. 5: 36 If you do not believe His word, you will not get the results even though He was physically present with you and physically spoke these words to you. When He was physically on earth, He could not perform many miracles in certain cities because of unbelief:

"And He did not many mighty works there BECAUSE OF THEIR UNBELIEF" Matt. 13: 58

So the key thing is speaking His word in FAITH. It really helps when you see the written word of God (scriptures) as if God were the one standing physically in front of you and speaking such words to you. And so when you come across a scripture like *"And the Lord shall make you the head and not the tail..."* Deut. 28: 13 do not regard it as just a mere statement of scripture. Just see God physically standing in front of you and speaking these words directly to you. Then it would be easier to have faith in His word and act out what His word says concerning you.

The words that proceed from the mouth of a believer go with power when spoken in FAITH. Scriptures say:

"Where the word of a king is there is power (Heb. "authority"), and who can say to him, what are you doing?" Eccle. 8: 4

And Jesus

"Has made us (believers) KINGS and priests to His God and Father..." Rev. 1: 6

God has also said that

"(All of) you are gods, and all of you are sons of the Most High" Psa. 82: 6

And that

"...just as you have spoken in my ears (in my hearing), so will I ASSUREDLY do to you" Num. 14: 28

Now that you are born again, you know that as a king whose words go with power, you should choose your words very circumspectly because God is waiting to act upon it. When you speak the word of God to your life and to that of others, God will be faithfully to it. You can make your future beautifully by the words you speak into it right now. You can also ruin it by the hopeless words you speak to it or by the beautiful words you refuse to speak to it.

I have prayerfully selected certain scripture verses to help in certain challenging moments you may face. Let them dwell richly in your spirit and meditate on them. Let your spirit be a storehouse for God's word, where you can access anytime and anywhere, and extract any word and speak it in faith to any obstacle that confronts you. His word never fails. Isai. 34: 16 No situation can resist the word of God. It is all-powerful. It is like fire and like hammer that breaks the rocks in pieces. Jer. 23: 29 What can withstand the word of the One who created the entire universe? He is Yahweh, the God of all flesh, and there is nothing impossible for Him to do. It was His word that raised the dead, healed the sick of all manner of incurable diseases, made the crippled walk, made the blind to see and the deaf to hear. People were delivered by His word. Demons heard His word and did the 100 meters dash! He sent His word and healed them, and delivered them from their destructions. Psa. 107: 20 It was His word (and the Holy Spirit) that created man. It is His word and the Holy Spirit that sustains every believer on earth today. It was the power of His word that mesmerized Pharaoh and the entire Egypt with signs and wonders. When God commissioned Moses to go into Egypt and liberate His people, the Israelites from the bondage to which the Egyptians had placed them, Moses gave the excuse of being a stutterer. God could have at this point allowed him to go into Egypt with His rod only but without speaking His word. But He knew the importance of His spoken word if Moses was to effectively stand before Pharaoh and the whole Egypt and bring liberation to His people. And so He commissioned Aaron the brother of Moses to accompany him to Egypt and be his mouth piece before Pharaoh (ref. Exodus 3 and 4). God's word is our medicine in all dimensions- physically, spiritually, emotionally, and mentally, and you must be compliant with this medicine to obtain the results you desire.

1. When you need healing, read: **Isaiah 53:4, 5; Psalm 105: 37; Isaiah 58: 6- 8; Psalm 30: 2; Isaiah 33: 24; Psalm 107: 20; Isaiah 30: 26.**

2. When you need deliverance, read: **Job 5: 19- 27; Jeremiah 1: 19; Jeremiah 20: 11; Psalm 91: 3; Obadiah 1: 17; Isaiah 61: 1; Isaiah 49: 24- 26; Psalm 50: 14, 15; Psalm 34: 17- 19; Psalm 33: 17- 19. Psalm 37: 39, 40.**

3. When you face fears, read: **Isaiah 51: 12- 16; Isaiah 41: 13, 14; Proverbs 29: 25; Psalms 46: 1- 3.**

4. When you face lack, read: **Psalm 34: 10; Philippians 4: 6, 19; Psalm 23: 1; Psalm 84: 11.**

5. When you face anxiety or worry, read: **Matthew 6: 25- 34; Philippians 4: 6; 1 Peter 5: 7; Psalm 55: 22; Psalm 37: 8.**

6. When you need strength, read: **Isaiah 41: 10, 15, 16; Psalm 18: 32- 34; Philippians 4: 13; Psalm 84: 5, 7; Psalm 138: 3; Isaiah 40: 28- 31.**

7. When you need protection, read: **2 Thessalonians 3: 3; Psalm 91; 1 John 5: 18; Isaiah 43: 2; Isaiah 51: 15, 16; Isaiah 54: 15, 17; Isaiah 59: 19; Psalm 84: 11; Deuteronomy 20: 4.**

8. When doubts to your salvation arise, read: **1 John 5: 11- 13; Romans 8: 16.**

9. When you are reminded of your past sins, read: **2 Corinthians 5: 17; Isaiah 43: 25; Isaiah 44: 22; Psalm 103: 12; Jeremiah 31: 34.**

10. When you are faced with negative thoughts, read: **Philippians 4: 8.**

11. When you feel lonely, dejected, abandoned, or depressed, read: **Hebrews 13: 4, 5; Isaiah 43: 2; Isaiah 41: 10; Isaiah 44: 21; Isaiah 49: 14- 16.**

12. When you are pressed about with trials, read: **Isaiah 43: 2; Romans 8: 28; 1 Corinthians 10: 13; James 1: 12.**

13. When you need direction, read: **Isaiah 30: 21; Psalm 27: 11; Proverbs 3: 5, 6.**

14. When doubts to answered prayers arise, read: **1 John 5: 14, 15; John 16: 24; Matthew 7: 7; Matthew 21: 22; John 14: 13, 14; Jeremiah 33: 3; Isaiah 55: 6.**

15. When you need upliftment, read: **Isaiah 49: 7; Isaiah 54: 2, 3; Isaiah 60: 1- 9.**

16. When you face sorrow or sadness, read: **Psalm 16: 11; Psalm 30: 4, 5; 2 Corinthians 6: 10; 2 Corinthians 7: 4; Psalm 126: 5;Isaiah 35: 10; Jeremiah 31: 11- 14; John 16: 20- 22.**

17. When you need peace, read: **Isaiah 26: 3; Philippians 4: 6, 7; John 14: 27; John 16: 33; Jeremiah 29: 11; Leviticus 26: 3, 6.**

18. When you feel you cannot hold on to the faith to the end, read: **Philippians 1: 6; Romans 14: 4; 1 Peter 1: 5; Hebrews 7: 25.**

19. When you need victory, read: **Romans 8: 31, 37; Psalm 28: 7; Philippians 4: 13; Deuteronomy 20: 4.**

20. When situations put in doubt God's love for you, read: **Romans 5: 6, 8; Romans 8: 38, 39; Job 7: 17, 18.**

Chapter 16

The Friend Who Never Looked Back

At The Garden of Gethsemane
(Matt. 26: 36- 56; Mrk. 14: 32- 52;
Luk. 22: 39- 53; Jhn. 18: 1- 11)

*H*ere the agony of Jesus truly began. On descending from the Mount of Olives into its valley, Jesus and His disciples entered the Garden of Gethsemane to pray. The prophecies made concerning His sufferings by the prophets of the Old Testament were about to be completed. Previously, His concerns had been with His disciples and believers to come in the world hence His prayer in John 17. But now His present concern was the terrible bodily and mental sufferings that lay ahead. On reaching Gethsemane, the burden on His spirit was already unbearable. His sorrow was beyond description; it was comparable to death itself. ^{Mrk. 14: 33, 34} He knew He had to pass through it if salvation for man was to be made possible. Taking Peter, James, and John, He retreated into the deeper and remote parts of the garden. Then also leaving these three behind, He went a little further and sank to the ground in lonely agony, and with mighty tears and crying He poured out His soul to God His Father who was able to save Him from death, ^{Heb. 5: 7} to let the cup of sufferings pass away from Him. He however surrendered His will to that of His Father's, so that His Father's will might take prominence. So distressed was Jesus that while praying, His sweat was like great drops of blood falling to the ground. Medically, this rare but serious condition is called "Haemohidrosis". It results from states of extreme emotional stress, anxiety or mental pressure. The tiny blood capillaries of the skin become dilated and weakened, thus permitting blood to percolate through the sweat pores and emerge with the sweat. In severe cases, the individual bled to death or went into a state of shock. Returning to the three disciples, He found them fast asleep. They were deeply overwhelmed with sorrow and could not even tarry with Him for an hour. He admonished them to watch and pray to avoid falling into temptation. Returning to pray, He was divinely strengthened by an angel from heaven. He had found victory in prayer and was now prepared for the great moment of the cross that lay ahead. Meanwhile, two more times did the disciples fall asleep rather than watch and pray with Him. At the moment of victory in prayer, His betrayer Judas Iscariot had arrived to deliver Him into the hands of His enemies.

Deserted By His Very Own Disciples

As He spoke with His sleepy disciples, the light of torches and lanterns could be seen. These were carried by a great multitude along with swords and staves. Matt. 26: 47 The great multitude were made up of a cohort of Roman soldiers (about 400- 600 men) who were released by Pilate, the Roman procurator of Judea, to the chief priests. This great number was requested because they thought the popularity of Jesus might cause some people to rise up to His rescue. Also part of this multitude were some chief priests, elders, and temple officers who were earlier sent to arrest Jesus but were rather overcome by His teachings. Jhn. 7: 32- 46 These men were sent by the Sanhedrin and were led by Judas who knew this secret place where Jesus was wont to praying and resting. They had previously attempted to capture Him openly, but feared public revolt. Nevertheless, just when they thought their hopes of ever seizing Him was dashed, it was given a breath of life when Judas, one of Jesus' disciples came up to them secretly and agreed to betray his master for a token fee (thirty pieces of silver, about 54 US dollars or 8,000 naira at today's market price). So appallingly, this fee was the standard price set for slaves in Israel by Moses. Exod. 21: 32 He laid out the plan himself as he knew the location of his master Jesus. Jesus knew by the Holy Spirit that Judas was to betray Him and He therefore made several attempts to dissuade him from committing such heinous sin. However, the treacherous mind of Judas was long made up. Not even His master stooping so low to wash his feet could elicit some sympathy and break his wicked heart. The final attempt by Jesus to save him was when He openly announced that one of His disciples would betray Him. To dissuade him further, He gave the very terrible consequence of such an act – it were better Judas was not born at all. ^{Matt. 26: 24} Judas knew very well that Jesus was referring to him, but still he hardened his heart. At this point, there was nothing else Jesus could do, rather than to tell him to carry out his treacherous act without delay. Satan then had his way in Judas, who got up and left the gathering of Jesus and His disciples for the last supper, so as to finalize his plans.

In the garden, while leading the band of armed men to Jesus, the sign for which Jesus was to be identified and seized was a kiss on the cheek. With a show of friendship, he approached Jesus and greeted Him as master with a kiss. The soldiers now receiving the signal advanced to take Jesus but were driven back and fell to the ground by a supernatural power. This showed that Jesus only surrendered Himself voluntarily to them; they had no power over Him. He submitted Himself to be seized and bound. All His disciples fled, leaving Him all alone. ^{Matt. 26: 56} John Mark, who at this time was not yet a disciple of Jesus, was awakened from his sleep by the noise near his house of the multitude proceeding to seize Jesus. In curiosity, he hurriedly followed them adorned in only a linen cloth. He observed as they seized and bound Jesus. Then being suspected to be one of the disciples, he was taken hold of. He however struggled to free himself and then fled naked, leaving his cloth behind. ^{Mrk. 14: 50} These fulfilled the prophecy in Zechariah 13: 7,

"Strike the shepherd and the sheep will scatter."

This arrest took place at midnight Wednesday.

The Trial Before The Sanhedrin (Unjust and Unfair) (Matt. 26: 57- 75; 27: 1- 10; Mrk. 14: 53- 72; 15: 1; Luk. 22: 54- 71; Jhn. 18: 12- 27)

The trial of Jesus can be described as a conspiracy by those who were expected to uphold justice. Those that wanted Him dead were the judges of His case. After His arrest, Jesus was immediately taken to the house of Caiaphas the high priest where members of the Sanhedrin had already gathered in anticipation of His arrest. The Sanhedrin was the Supreme Court of the Jews and was composed of 71 members including the High Priest who was president of this council, chief priests, scribes and elders. Jesus was first led before Annas, the father in- law to Caiaphas the High Priest. Annas, even though deposed as high priest at this time, still had a great influence within the Sanhedrin. This was why he was still regarded as the high priest. He and his son Caiaphas were Sadducees. During His interview with Annas, Jesus was struck by an officer but He endured it with all humility. After the brief interview with Annas, He was transferred to Caiaphas. When presented before Caiaphas and the Sanhedrin, the cohort of Roman soldiers returned to their quarters. At least 23 members of the Sanhedrin were required for a quorum. This Jewish trial of Jesus was unlawful and had many irregularities. Some of the illegalities included:

1. The trial was conducted and continued through out the night. Conducting capital trials at night was forbidden by Jewish customs.

2. When an individual charged with a crime was presented, the council first focused on evidences that would acquit him, before they focused on evidences that would indict him. In the case of Jesus they focused first and only on the accusations that would indict Him for a crime leading to death.

3. Some of the judges of His case took part and masterminded His arrest. This was contrary to Jewish law that required the judges of a case to be neutral.

4. He was interrogated (by Annas) before the main trial commenced, in order to get indicting statements from Him.

5. In cases heard, at least two witnesses were needed to corroborate the exact accusation against the defendant. Deut. 17:6 In the case of Jesus, several people brought some accusations, but no two witnesses ever accused Him of the same crime.

6. During the trial at the house of Caiaphas, the indicting crime was blasphemy. Mrk. 14: 63, 64 However, before Pilate, He was accused of sedition against Caesar Tiberius, and of refusing to pay taxes to Caesar. Luk. 23: 2

7. In the open, the council was supposed to hear accusations presented by witnesses and not to initiate the accusations themselves. In the case of Jesus, they initiated the accusations against Him and propelled them.

8. They delivered a guilty verdict at the end of the night session, without allowing a day's break.

9. The chief priests and the whole council who were the judges in the case sought false witness against Jesus so they might

condemn Him to death. ^{Matt. 26: 59} Such witnesses usually took a solemn oath at the court to tell the truth. It is horrible to even think that it was the high priest, who hired these false witnesses, that administered such an oath.

After the trial, Jesus was adjudged worthy of death and He was then spat upon several times. The servants even struck Him with their palms, blindfolded Him and severely mocked Him. ^{Mrk. 14: 65; Matt. 26: 68} Many other blasphemous things were said against Him which are not recorded. ^{Luk. 22: 65} Then with more blows, He was led.

In order to add legality to the scandalous trial held at night, a formal assembly of the council took place in the morning. This was merely to confirm the verdict already reached at in the night.

Denial of Peter

While Jesus was taken to the house of Caiaphas, Peter had secretly followed them afar off, and gained entry into the court in the house through John, the beloved disciple who was known to the attendants at the court. From his position in the court, Peter could watch the proceedings of the trial of His master. When recognized by some people within the building as a disciple of Jesus on several occasions, three times he denied ever knowing or associating with Jesus. In fact, on the third occasion, he cursed and swore ever knowing Jesus. ^{Mrk. 14: 66- 72} At this instant, Jesus turned and looked at Him, a look so full of grief and disappointment which could never be forgotten. Peter in deep repentance, went out and wept bitterly.

Trial before Pilate

In the trial before the Jews, Jesus was condemned to death. Now the Jews could condemn to death, but they did not have the power to execute the sentence. This power, which was taken from them, was now vested in the Roman procurator who at this point in time was Pontius Pilate. Jesus was therefore taken to this man, ruthless but weak in resolve, in the hope of the Jews persuading him to pronounce the death sentence on Jesus. The residential palace (Praetorium) of Pilate in Jerusalem was the former palace of Herod the Great. Jesus was taken to the judgment hall of the Praetorium at about 6 a.m. Thursday morning. His accusers however remained outside the palace because they refused to defile themselves by entering the palace of a heathen and so render themselves unfit to eat Passover.

The accusers first brought a charge of blasphemy against Jesus. Jesus was silent on these accusations and Pilate, after cross- examining Him, found no wrong in Him. Knowing that Pilate would not grant their wishes on mere charges of blasphemy which had to do with Jewish laws and not Roman laws, the accusers decided to bring up charges that were directly related to Roman laws for which they expected Pilate to have no choice but grant their wish. They now accused Him of forbidding the payment of taxes to Caesar (which was a false accusation) and claiming to be a king. Having heard these, Pilate considered them, especially the last charge too serious to be overlooked. He went back into the Praetorium and examined Jesus on the charges but also found no crime in Him. Jhn. 18: 38 This was a statement of acquittal and according to Roman laws, this should have ended the trial and secured the immediate discharge of Jesus. But the clamour by the Jews for His death mounted and fresh accusations were volleyed against Him. On hearing an accusation that had to do with His teaching in Galilee, Pilate not wanting to have a hand in the death of the innocent man, referred Him for trial to Herod Antipas, the ruler of Galilee who was coincidentally in Jerusalem for the celebration of the Passover feast. However, Herod, not interested in the case but in miracles which he had long expected Jesus to perform for him but to no avail, Luk. 9: 9 mocked Him and sent Him back to Pilate. Both men who hitherto had been inherent enemies now became friends. Luk. 23: 12

Now Pilate in another resolve to free Jesus summoned the chief priests and this time, he involved the people. He openly acknowledged the innocence of Jesus and in accordance with a Jewish custom of releasing a prisoner at the Passover feast, he offered them a choice of whom he should set free between Jesus Christ, an innocent man, and Barabbas, a notorious criminal. He thought the crowd would opt for a harmless Jesus. But he was so wrong. The chief priests secretly within this crowd disillusioned their minds against Jesus and canvassed their support for the release of the criminal Barabbas and destruction of Jesus. Pilate's wish to release Jesus was further strengthened by a message he received from his wife who had a dream about Jesus and warned him to have nothing to do with the righteous man. Matt. 27: 19 The crowd cried for the release of Barabbas and crucifixion of Jesus, whom they called "this man". Luk. 23: 18- 23

In a last attempt to free Jesus, Pilate had Him scourged and allowed his soldiers place a crown of thorns upon His head, array Him in purple robe and mock Him as king of the Jews. He afterwards presented the severely chastised Jesus who was bleeding to the crowd, with the thought that once they saw how he had been brutally chastised, their hearts would instantly melt with pity and they would request His release. But this only succeeded in serving as an appetizer to the blood –thirsty crowd. They wanted to see more than that- they wanted Him dead; they wanted Him crucified. As a last resort to make the unyielding Pilate grant their wish, they threatened that if he released Jesus, he was not a friend of Caesar but a friend of the one who made Himself a king in defiance of Caesar. This finally weakened the resolve of Pilate to free Jesus, as he knew the people could charge him before Caesar with the very grave crime of condoning treason. This could cost him his office and even his very life.

Finally succumbing to their threats, he washed his hands off he innocent blood of Jesus, and the people shouted vehemently in unison,

"His blood be on us and on our children!" Matt. 27: 25

Taking his place on the judgment seat, he passed the sentence for Jesus to be crucified. This was midnight, Thursday, April 13.

The Scourging

Scourging was a prelude for every criminal that was condemned to be crucified. The only people exempted from this were Roman citizens and women. A scourge was made up of a handle from which emerged about 12 leather cords called flagellum (plural "flagella"). At the end of these cords were attached small pieces of jagged bone and a heavy metal which made each strike more excruciating and caused the victim to bleed profusely. The Jewish law required that the number of stripes brought about by this whip was not to exceed forty. To avoid inadvertently exceeding this number which was to be strictly adhered to, the number of stripes was reduced to thirty- nine. Deut. 25: 3; 2 Cor. 11: 23- 25 This was the Jewish law but not Roman. As such, the Romans always exceeded the required number of thirty- nine according to the Jewish law. Many victims before reaching the cross went into states of unconsciousness and even died from the scourge alone.

After the death sentence from Pilate, Jesus was taken by the Roman soldiers into the Praetorium where the cruel mockery was resumed in an intensified form. He was tied to a vertical post upon which His robe was stripped off Him to expose His body. Two Roman soldiers were assigned to Him to execute the scourging. Then the torture began. With each blow, a part of His skin was ripped out of His body. As the blows continued, deeper parts of the skin became involved. When two consecutive strikes hit the same stripe on His back, the wounds were made deeper. In fact the wounds were described as being like the long and deep furrows made in a farm field during preparation of the soil for cultivation. [Psa. 129: 3] It got so deep that the deep back muscles were breached and torn apart. Chunks of His flesh littered the ground and the bleeding became so profuse that His blood adorned the ground. His abdomen was not also spared. When these two soldiers got exhausted, two additional soldiers came in to replace them. They continued the scourging until Jesus collapsed to the ground, bathed in His own blood. Not yet done with Him, He was lifted up and ropes were then used to hold Him on to the post. This horrifying torture continued intermittently through out the night until the completely battered Jesus was let off. This was certainly the moment of the powers of darkness. [Luk. 22: 53] It is not certain how many whips He received, but if He had been whipped fifty times at one instance, which was more than likely, it meant that He received fifty times twelve stripes. That is, six hundred stripes. Considering that this torture went on through out the night, one can only imagine the number of stripes He received. All these fulfilled scripture which said,

"By His stripes we are healed" [Isai. 53: 5]

Because of the deep penetrating wounds inflicted, severe blood loss was a typical feature of scourging, especially one as severe as that of Jesus. The wounds penetrated as far as the muscles of the back, tearing them and even exposing the bones. The victims were cruelly weakened by this, and this act alone ensured that they did not survive long when crucified. With a crown of thorns placed upon His head, Jesus was adorned with a purple (scarlet) robe and a reed was mockingly thrust into His hand as a scepter. The crown of thorns when placed upon His head produced a gush of blood from the head. The scalp of the head is about the most vascularized area of the human body, and a slight injury could produce excessive blood loss that could be dangerous. This contributed to a progressively weakening state and eventually shock would gradually set in. The crown of thorns and scarlet robe used to adorn Jesus has some biblical significance. Thorns in scripture metaphorically signify the curse of man. [Gen. 3: 18] It became existent only after the fall of man through sin. Scarlet as used in Isaiah 1: 18 signifies sin. A comparison is made between it and the snow (which signifies purity), showing that these two are extremes. Scarlet is used to describe a permanent and extreme form of sin. Thus, Jesus Christ was crowned with the curse of man and adorned with the sins of the world, even the very worst of sins which though considered indelible like scarlet, was made as white as snow by Him.

With these, Jesus was now left at the mercy of the whole band of Roman soldiers who spat on Him in deep hatred and struck Him on the head several times with the reed placed in His hand. ^{Mrk. 15: 19} His beard was also plucked out. ^{Isa. 50: 6} After all these, the scarlet robe was taken off Him and His own garments were put on Him in preparation for the end. He was so battered and marred beyond human form and recognition that He was hardly recognized when led out to be crucified. He was so appalling to behold. All these events fulfilled what was written in scripture concerning Him:

"I gave my back to the smiters, and my cheeks to them that plucked off the hair. I hid not my face from shame and spitting.

As many were amazed at you; His appearance was so marred more than any man, and His shape more than the sons of men.

But He was wounded because of our transgressions and crushed (Heb. "daka" meaning "to be beaten to pieces") because of our depravities. The discipline (chastisement; punishment) for our peace (Heb. "shalom" meaning "complete wellbeing", and not just "tranquility of mind") was upon Him, and with His stripes we are healed" ^{Isaiah 50: 6; 52: 14; 53: 5}

Jesus passed through the most frightful physical exhaustion, mental strain, agony of scourging, suffering from wounds of the dreadful night and morning, with complete courage and unembittered spirit. He could have turned His back on it but He had to face it for the sake of the world. He humbly submitted Himself to this cup which the Father had given Him to drink to make the salvation of man possible. It is very touching to think that even in this terrible hour and sufferings He faced, His main focus was to restore fallen man to His original position and save them from destruction. His love for man even while in deep agony was unbreakable. It is a sight to move the stoniest of hearts. The strength won through prayer at the Garden of Gethsemane had brought Him steadfast peace, which could not be altered even by the greater sufferings that lay ahead at the cross.

The Journey To Calvary

The path Jesus made to Calvary (Grk. "**Golgotha**") was strewn by His bleeding stripes and His strong heart broken tears. Every condemned criminal had to carry His own cross naked from the point of scourging to the site of crucifixion. It was either the entire cross or more frequently, only the horizontal crossbar (called the **patibulum**), that was carried. The whole cross (patibulum plus the vertical post called the **stipes**) weighed much more, thus making it difficult for any one to carry the entire cross. The site of crucifixion was typically outside the city for several reasons, mainly sanitary. The crucified victims were at times left to decompose on the cross and thus there was a possibility that it could defile the people in consonance with the Law of Moses. More so, crucified victims whether dead or alive on the cross, were vulnerable to being eaten up by wild beasts, birds of prey and insects, and this would constitute a nuisance in the city.

The patibulum was fixed across the shoulders and nape of Jesus' neck and ropes were used to support the patibulum to His shoulders. A profusely bleeding Jesus had to trudge with the cross from the site of scourging (Praetorium) to the site of crucifixion (Calvary), a distance of about 650 meters. As He staggered along, His blood filled the entire path to Calvary, physically exhausted from the scourging and from lack of food and sleep since Gethsemane (a period of about two days), and emotionally and mentally distressed from all the spiritual battles and obstacles that were laid in His way to kill Him before He reached the cross, which was the defining moment that would save man and reconcile him to God. As He staggered down a stairway just outside the gate that led to Calvary, Jesus, possibly fainting under this burden, fell to the ground facedown with the entire weight of the patibulum on Him. He possibly ruptured an internal organ from this. It was at this point that a stranger, Simon from Cyrene was summoned to carry the cross to the site of crucifixion. [Matt. 27: 32]

The Crucifixion of Jesus

Crucifixion was the most horrible, painful and the most degrading capital punishment which the cruelty of a most cruel age could ever devise. It was reserved for the worst crimes and for the lowest class of people. It was the perfect form of torture and punishment that brought slow but extremely painful death. So humiliating was death on a cross that it is summed up in a Roman proverb:

"Let the very name of the cross be far away not only from the body of a Roman citizen, but even from his thoughts, his eyes, his ears."

Death on a cross was also greatly detested by the Jews because *"cursed is everyone that hangs on a tree".* Gal. 3: 13; Deut. 21: 23 Yet they hounded Pilate to mete it out on one of their own.

The victims of crucifixion literally died a thousand deaths. The suffering was intense, especially in hot climates. Inflammation around nailed wounds produced fever, which was made worse by body strain, extreme thirst, and exposure to the heat of the sun. Tearing of the nerves by the nails produced searing pains. Engorgement of the arteries of the head produced insufferable throbbing headaches. Tetanus was also frequent. The rigors that accompanied it caused tearing of the flesh around the nailed wounds, and so aggravated the agony. The mind was extremely confused and anxious. Respiratory distress was grave. These continued until the victims became unconscious and died.

The crucifixion of Jesus took place at about 9 a.m. Friday, April 14. When He arrived the site of crucifixion, the patibulum was set on the ground and the garments of Jesus were forcefully stripped off Him. This could have caused more pain and bleeding because by this time, the coagulated blood from His stripes would be adherent to His garments. He was compellingly pushed to the ground, His back down and His arms outstretched across the patibulum. This act would have caused dizziness and disorientation because of postural hypotension due to severe blood loss from the scourging. Before the actual crucifixion began, Jesus was offered a drink of strong wine mixed with myrrh. This served as an analgesic to crucified victims. He however refused the drink after tasting it and chose to face the pain of the cross to the full. With this, the crucifixion began properly. With the outstretched arm, nails about 5 to 7 inches long and 3/8 inch in diameter were placed at His wrists and with ruthless strikes of a mallet, they were driven right through his wrists and on to the wooden patibulum. Because of their location at the middle of the forearm, the median nerves (the major nerve supply to the hand, forearm, and arm) were crushed. This produced waves of excruciating pains that radiated up the arm. In addition, it was highly possible that some bones of the wrists (carpals) were fractured by the nails, thus producing intense periosteal (bone) pains. Unlike scourging, crucifixion especially of the hands was relatively bloodless because of the more peripheral location of the blood vessels. However, it was much more excruciating. With the aid of ropes, the victim was then lifted up to the top of the vertical post of the cross (stipes). The stipes was permanently located at the crucifixion site, and it weighed about 86kg. About half way up the stipes was the **sedile**, a support on to which the feet of the victim was nailed. It was when being lifted upon the cross that Jesus uttered the touching prayer and His first word on the cross:

"Father, forgive them; for they do not know what they do" Luk. 23:34

His feet were then placed on the sedile. Because the length of the victim's legs usually exceeded the location of the sedile, the legs had to be flexed and rotated laterally, after which one foot was placed upon the other and both were nailed to the sedile. Jesus was crucified alongside two criminals, one to His left and the other to His right. Nailing of the feet unlike those of the hands was a very bloody and painful process. It produced rupture to the ***dorsalis pedis*** blood vessels that supply the feet and crushing of the deep peroneal nerves producing searing pains. As the stipes balanced on the ground vertically from a near horizontal position, this produced searing pain around the nailed areas of the hands and feet. During and after crucifixion, Jesus suffered mockery from the soldiers, the chief priests and even the dying criminals. One of them was touched by the holiness and meekness of Jesus even in the face of death and mockery, and he repented of his act. The response of Jesus to this penitent criminal was even more touching and far more than this criminal had expected. Jesus, while gasping for breath uttered,

"Today, you will be with me in paradise" Luk. 23:43

It was His second word on the cross. Standing near the cross were some women, among whom was His mother Mary who was deeply heartbroken. She was being comforted by John, the beloved disciple. Seeing them, He lovingly committed His mother to the care of John, saying to Mary,

"Woman, behold your son," and to John, **"behold, your mother."**
Jhn. 19: 26, 27

This was His third word on the cross. He was offered wine vinegar by the soldiers (the second drink offered Him). Luk. 23: 36 In His presence, His outer garment was divided by the soldiers and since the inner garment could not be divided because of the nature of its material and weaving, lots had to be cast for it. This fulfilled Psalm 22: 18:

"They part my garments among themselves, and cast lots upon my vesture"

Let us now for a moment consider some of the sufferings of Jesus from the crucifixion and scourging from a medical point of view.

1. **Respiratory Distress.** This was perhaps the most distressing of all. In normal individuals, inspiration is an active process, requiring effort, while expiration is a passive (effortless) process. In crucified victims it was the reverse – inspiration became passive and expiration became active. This was due to the following – on crucifixion, the entire weight of the victim's body was directed downwards towards the sedile. This caused a downward pull of the body on the arms and shoulders, which became stretched up and outwards. This up and outward stretch of the arms and shoulders in turn caused a stretch of the intercostals muscles (major muscles of inspiration) and other accessory muscles of respiration (such as the pectoralis major and minor, and the scalenii muscles). This stretch kept them in a fixed state of inspiration – the thoracic cavity was also expanded by this upward stretch and this facilitated passive inspiration. A reason why inspiration is active in normal individuals is because the small volume and consequently high pressure of the thoracic cavity poses a resistance to intake of air which would require much effort to overcome. In the stretched state, the volume of this cavity is dramatically increased and the pressure is reduced, thus facilitating passive intake of air. Because of the fixed state of the muscles of inspiration, the respiratory muscles hardly ever came into play. Thus, the entire burden of expiration was placed on the less efficient diaphragm muscles. The diaphragm only allows for shallow breathing unlike the intercostals muscles which allowed for a deeper and more effective form of breathing when contracting and relaxing. Because of this shallow form of breathing, carbon dioxide concentration in the body soon rose up to dangerous levels in the body (medically called "**hypercarbia**"). Carbon dioxide is a waste product of the body's metabolic processes and has

to be eliminated from the body. This can be done only in the presence of efficient respiration (deep and full respiration) and not shallow respiration. As carbon dioxide levels keep building up in the face of shallow breathing, muscle cramps and difficult breathing (medically called "**dyspnoea**") begin to set in. Even more, the pain around the wrist was aggravated by the up and outward stretch of the arm.

To exhale properly, the victim had to firmly place his nailed feet on the sedile and use it to haul up his body. This manoeuvre causes the previously outstretched arms and shoulders to become flexed at the elbows. This further caused a relaxation of the intercostals and accessory respiratory muscles which allowed for proper expiration of carbon dioxide. This manoeuvre produced excruciating pain in the nailed feet and hands as they were rotated about the nails. The back of the victim, which had earlier been scourged, would also scrape against the rough wooden stipes as he hauled up his body in an attempt to properly exhale. This would cause reopening and rebleeding of the wounds obtained during the scourge.

With the body lifted up by its weight placed on the feet, respiration became a lot easier. However, the pain in the nailed part of the feet became increasingly excruciating because it now supported the body's weight to aid proper respiration. This severe pain caused the victim to slump down again, thus taking the arms and shoulders to their previous stretched out state. The intercostals and accessory respiratory muscles became fixed in an inspiratory state again and respiratory distress set in again. When the carbon dioxide concentration rose to an intolerable level, he again hauled up his body using his feet to support the body weight. These manoeuvres continued until the victim became exhausted, slipped into unconsciousness and died. In order to hasten the victim's death, the Roman soldiers would break the legs of the victim just below the knee joint or dislocate the shoulder joint by striking the arm with a heavy mallet or a similar tool. When the legs were broken, it became impossible for the victim to haul up his body and support his body weight on his feet to aid respiration. The respiratory muscles therefore remained in a fixed state of inspiration and breathing was continually shallow. Carbon dioxide levels built up and this resulted in muscle cramps, dyspnoea, throbbing headaches, dizziness and disorientation. If the arms were not broken, the victim then as a last resort used the muscles of the arms and shoulders to haul up his body slightly. This however never lasted long as the shallow breathing alongside the fatigued muscles of the arms and shoulders, and the body generally caused rapid asphyxiation. The victim thus died of suffocation.

It is worth mentioning the aspect of speech in regard to crucifixion. Speech is facilitated by respiration; it is carried out during the expiratory phase. Speech was therefore near to impossible in crucified victims. The only period they could speak was when they hauled up their bodies with the aid of their feet on the sedile because it was at this stage that respiration was easier. But they had to endure extreme pains to do this. The fiery pains they experienced by these manoeuvrings made it difficult to utter even a word from the cross. Thus the seven times our Lord Jesus spoke from the cross is very understandable, considering also the deep agony, physical torture and exhaustion, mental and emotional distress He had faced before this. He spoke these seven times out of great pain and respiratory difficulty, and only when He had manoeuvred Himself (by hauling Himself up) to the position where He could speak. The words spoken from the cross were indeed very special.

2. **Hypovolemia and Haemoconcentration.** The hypovolemia (reduced circulating blood volume) suffered by Jesus was as a result of the scourging He had received, thirst from all the agony, and partly to the crucifixion. Hypovolemic shock then set in. The kidneys as a result were unable to adequately compensate for the acidosis precipitated by the hypercarbia. Soon enough, fluid began to seep out of the now permeable blood capillaries and into the extravascular space, leading to a state of haemoconcentration (a condition in which the blood cells are relatively higher than the volume of plasma needed for them to circulate). Concomitantly the pericardial and pleural spaces began to fill with serum (pericardial and pleural

effusion, respectively). The pericardial space is the potential space between the heart and its covering (the pericardium). In this state of effusion, the normal contractile activity of the heart is disrupted because the fluid that accumulates affects the contraction and relaxation of the heart. This leads to fatal arrhythmias, acute heart failure, myocardial infarction and rupture. Pleural space and effusions are similar to those of the heart. In this case, the lungs are involved. The failing heart (due to pericardial effusion) now had to perform greater work in pushing the thick blood (due to haemoconcentration) through a wider systemic circulation. This increased its stress and caused fatal arrhythmias. The inability to compensate led to further hypoxia (reduced oxygen supply) to tissues, greater pericardial and pleural effusions which further compressed the heart, and increased acidosis. All these eventually resulted in death due to acute heart failure, fatal cardiac arrhythmias or cardiac arrest in addition to the asphyxia from respiratory distress. Thus, death from crucifixion resulted from diverse aetiologies.

3. **Hyperpyrexia (Fever).** This is an increase in the normal temperature of the body. This was due to varied causes including the excruciating pain following severance of the nerves of the hands and feet, thirst, local inflammation at the nailed hands and feet, physical stress, and prolonged exposure to heat of the sun.

Death of Jesus

1. **Spiritual Death.** Three hours had now elapsed since His crucifixion; it was now midday. The mockery of Jesus that had continued unabated these three hours suddenly began to die away as an astonishing natural change occurred. The sun became dark and refused to give out its light, and deep darkness covered the land for about three hours. It seemed like nature itself was horror-struck at the grand injustice that was committed and hid itself in protest. Right in heaven, God the Father was deeply agonized and grieved at the pains and sufferings of His dear Son. Heaven stood still. Spiritually, the

entire sins of the world were upon Jesus and God the Father had to turn His holy face away from His Beloved Son. This was the most painful moment for Jesus. Never in His entire life had His fellowship with His dear Father been interrupted. Now for the first time in His entire life on earth, He felt so lonely. For the first time in His entire life, He was denied the comfort and warmth of His Father's presence. For the first time in His entire life, He experienced sin. He tasted this sin, not because He sinned but because it was placed upon Him so that the real culprit (man) could be free from its burden and consequences.

"...for He (Jesus) was cut off from the land of the living; for the transgressions of My people He was stricken.

And they made His grave with the wicked- but with the rich at death, because He had done no violence, nor was any deceit in His mouth.

Yet it pleased the Lord to crush Him; He has put Him to grief. When You make His soul an offering for sin, He shall see His seed, He shall prolong His days, and the pleasure of the Lord shall prosper in His hand" Isai. 53: 8- 10

Even those for whom He made the costly sacrifice had stood by to mock Him. In great depths of indescribable agony and loneliness, He made a sorrowful cry, His fourth from the cross:

"My God, my God, why have you forsaken me?" Matt. 27: 46

It was about 3 p.m. now, six hours after He was crucified. He had to face this painful experience of spiritual death for our salvation to become a reality. Very touchingly, even on the cross with all its humiliation, pain and cruelty, Jesus was more concerned for His malefactors.

2. **Physical Death.** Jesus had now been six hours on the cross and His condition progressively deteriorated. The end was now very near. The victim of crucifixion usually lingered in his agony for days, but the extreme strain on body and mind which Jesus had undergone the past few days ended His sufferings earlier. The darkness which covered the land was

now beginning to fade away, light was gradually returning and with it, peace. With that, He exclaimed, (His fifth word),

"I thirst!" Jhn. 19: 28

At this, He was offered vinegar by means of a sponge attached to a hyssop (His third drink on the cross). When He drank it, He cried out victoriously, with the consciousness that His work and purpose on earth had been accomplished,

"It is finished!" Jhn. 19: 30

It was His sixth memorable word from the cross. Calm and peace had returned, and they settled splendidly upon Him. His work of restoring man to his glorious position as God had originally created him, and reconciling him back to God, was achieved. He had won the battle for man. It cost Him so much but it was worth it. He had seen the travail of His soul for mankind and was satisfied. Isai. 53: 11 Then with a final loud cry, He committed His spirit to God,

"Father into your hands, I commend my spirit!" Luk. 23: 46

This was His seventh and last word from the cross. Following this, He quietly bowed His head and willingly surrendered Himself to death. He had laid down His soul on the altar of sacrifice for His sheep.

At His death, remarkable events occurred. The veil of the temple which separated the Most Holy Place (which was symbolically where the throne of God was) and the outer courts (which was where the people that came to worship were restricted) was torn from top to bottom. This was a sign that Jesus had opened up the way to the throne of God for every man. Heb. 9: 8, 12 Man now had access to God. A great earthquake also occurred which shook the city and tore the rocks apart. Many saints who had died were raised. Matt. 27: 52, 53 attesting to the resurrection power of Jesus, and His power over death.

With these events, the mood of onlookers changed. The power of the cross was brought to the fore. A dying criminal had been won on the cross. Now the Roman centurion who commanded the soldiers and the other onlookers confessed that Jesus was truly the Son of God. ^{Matt. 27: 54} The onlookers who had previously mocked Jesus, now left the scene, smiting their breasts in deep regret for the great misdeed that had been done.

Confirmation of Death

A quartenion of Roman soldiers were usually assigned to each crucified victim, and when the victim died, they were responsible for certifying the death of such victim. Now because crucified victims were forbidden to remain on the cross during special feasts such as Passover, the soldiers were requested to hasten the death of the three crucified victims. The following day which in Jewish time was to begin from sunset, about 6 p.m. that Friday, was the start of the special Jewish Passover. It was now 3 p.m., about three hours to the start of the Jewish Passover. The legs of the two criminals who were still alive at this moment were crushed with sledge hammers to hasten their death and thus end their sufferings. When they got to Jesus, they realized He was already dead and so there was no need to break His legs. This fulfilled the prophecy in Psalm 34: 20 which says,

"And none of His bones shall be broken."

Pilate was much surprised at the quick death of Jesus. Victims could survive as long as three days. To confirm the death of Jesus, a Roman soldier pierced His right side with a spear. The spear passed right through the intercostal space and into the right ventricle of the heart from where a sudden flow of blood and water (serum from pericardial effusion) occurred. Afterwards, Jesus was brought down and buried in a new tomb owned by Joseph of Arimathea, a hitherto secret disciple of His.

Resurrection

Precisely three days after He died on the cross, Jesus arose just as He had promised. He arose with victory over death, sin and the devil for everyone that would believe in Him and receive Him into their lives. In the intervening days between His burial and resurrection, the chief priests and Pharisees attempted to do all within their powers to stop the resurrection but only ended up confirming it. Jesus when alive had declared that He would die as scripture had foretold, but arise on the third day. ^{Luk. 18: 31- 33} The chief priests and Pharisees being jittery over this, and with the thought that the disciples might steal the body of Jesus and claim that He had risen from the dead, they went to Pilate and requested him for a watch of soldiers to guard the tomb of Jesus. To be doubly sure, they sealed the tomb with the official seal. All these efforts only succeeded in providing evidence for the resurrection, as Jesus arose from the dead by the power of the Holy Spirit.

The Great Commission

Jesus Christ, after His resurrection appeared unto many of His disciples. Now it was time to depart for heaven from where He came to secure the release of what herald the beginning of His church – the Holy Spirit. His job was done and He was to leave for the Holy Spirit to come down and continue through the disciples where He left off. Victory had been accomplished, salvation was won, the pain and agony was now past, and it was time to be glorified. He now finally met with His disciples, about five hundred ^{1 Cor. 15: 6} at the Mount of Olives to give His final instructions. At this, He gave the great commission, to make disciples of all the nations. ^{Matt. 28: 18- 20; Mrk. 16: 15} The Holy Spirit was to come and empower them to fulfill this very important commission, which applied to every believer. Having said all that He had to say, He was taken up into heaven in their sight while blessing them. He then sat at the right hand of God the Father. About ten days later, the Holy Spirit came down majestically to dwell in believers and continue the work of Jesus Christ in them. Just as Jesus had ascended into heaven, so would He come again to take His people (believers) to be with Him.

Chapter 17

To the Death

 common adage says, "He is no man who has not found what he can die for". The quality of what a man lays down his life for is very important. It shows how dear or valuable such a thing is to that fellow. Jesus Christ said that there is no greater love than when a man lays down his very life (Grk. "*psuche*"- "soul") for his friend. [Jhn. 15: 13] Jesus never just spoke it, but He acted it out at the cross of Calvary. And He left us with a new commandment-

"love one another; AS I HAVE LOVED YOU, so you also love one another." [Jhn. 13: 34; 15: 12; 1 Jhn. 3: 23; 2 Jhn. 1: 5]

In other words, our love for one another should just be as the love He had and still has for us. Since the love of Jesus Christ is very great, Jesus Christ was indirectly saying that we should love to the best that we can. Love is essential to be faithful even to the death. The wish of Jesus to see us redeemed from death and restored back to God the Father made Him face the cross, despite all its humiliation. We now look at a few of the disciples of Jesus who never cared so much about their lives but gave themselves for their master, even to the death. It brings to mind the French soldiers of the past who held the slogan "to the death". It meant they either won the battle or they died fighting. They were never to surrender in the battle field. They were prepared to die for their cause. This was the attitude of the disciples and this should be the attitude of every Christian. The disciples, once very faint- hearted had finally found something really worth giving up their lives for. It was Jesus Christ. Some even got exhilarated when they were persecuted, for they longed to suffer for Christ. Others wished they were taken away for the sake of Jesus. The only thing that seemed to have restrained them was the need for the dissemination of the gospel of salvation.

ANDREW

Before he met Jesus, he was a fisherman by profession. He was a brother to Peter. He laboured for the gospel of Christ in several regions including Macedonia (present day Greece), Asia Minor (present day Asian Turkey), Scythia (Moldova, Ukraine, and Eastern Russia), Thrace (parts of Greece, Bulgaria and Turkey), and Lydia (part of Turkey). It is said that while preaching in the region of Patras, Greece, the wife of the proconsul in this region got converted to Jesus and this offended the proconsul who had Apostle Andrew imprisoned. He was severely scourged and tied by ropes to an X- shaped cross where he remained, bleeding for two days. While on this cross, he still showed great love and concern for his malefactors by preaching the gospel of Christ and encouraging those around him. He continued this for two days before he went to be with the Lord Jesus. As the Lord came to take him home, he was surrounded by heavenly light and then he died. He died about 70 AD.

BARTHOLOMEW

He was also called Nathanael [Jhn. 1:45] and was the brother of Philip. He preached the gospel of salvation in India, Armenia, Phrygia (West Central Turkey), and Syria. While preaching in Albanopolis in Armenia, he was seized by King Astyages of Armenia and was beaten severely. His entire skin was removed from his body (a process called "flaying") and then he was crucified head down, and was lastly beheaded. He was the disciple that had initially doubted the Messiahship of Jesus, with the words,

"Can there any good thing come out of Nazareth?" [Jhn. 1:46]

JAMES THE SON OF ALPHAEUS

Also known as James "the less" or "little" in contrast to James the son of Zebedee. He was the brother of Judas (not Iscariot), Joses and Simon Zelotes, and was a cousin of Jesus. His father Alphaeus (Greek name for the Hebrew "Cleophas". See John 19: 25) married Mary, the sister of the Virgin

Mary. He was stoned to death by the Jews in Jerusalem for preaching the gospel of Christ and was buried close to the sanctuary.

JAMES THE BROTHER OF THE LORD

He was popularly called James "the just one" by the Jews after the resurrection of Jesus. James preached this gospel in Jerusalem. By his preaching, Piosbata, the wife of Ananus, who was at that time the acting governor of Jerusalem and High Priest, was separated from her husband. This inflamed him against James. He for that reason assembled the Sanhedrin of judges and had James and some of his companions brought before them. He then fabricated accusations against them as law breakers and delivered them to be stoned to death. This was during the Passover of AD 63. James was taken to the top of the temple in Jerusalem by the Scribes and Pharisees and was compelled to denounce his faith in Jesus and deny Him before the people in Jerusalem whom they said "were going astray after Jesus as though He were the Christ". Then in allusion to his prophecy on the coming of Christ Jesus, [James 5: 8, 9] they said, "Tell us, O just one, which is the door of Jesus?" James replied in the hearing of the people below, "Why ask ye me concerning Jesus, the Son of Man? He sitteth at the right hand of power, and will come again on the clouds of heaven." Most of the people cried "Hosanna to the Son of David."

Madly irritated at this, he was thrown down from the pinnacle of the temple tower, a height of about 100 feet (30 meters). He however survived the fall. Seeing he was still alive, they began to beat and stone him, but then he struggled to his knees and prayed the same prayer of forgiveness as Christ Jesus did on the cross- "Father, forgive them, for they know not what they do". One of the persecutors, being a fuller, took his fuller's club (similar to a baseball bat) which he used to beat out clothes, and with it he finally dashed out the brains of James. He was buried on the spot, by the temple. He was killed about AD 63, just before the destruction of Jerusalem which took place 7 years later. He wrote the epistle of James and was the president of the church council at Jerusalem. [Acts 12: 17; 15: 19; Gal. 2: 12]

JAMES THE SON OF ZEBEDEE

He was the brother of John and one of the three disciples that belong to the inner circle of Jesus. He was a fisherman before he was fully called to be a disciple of Jesus. His father was from the tribe of Levi (priestly line) while his mother was of the tribe of Judah (kingly line). Following the persecution of the early church, he moved out and preached the gospel in India with Peter, as well as in Spain. On visiting Jerusalem with Peter to observe the Passover in AD 44, he was seized and beheaded by King Agrippa I. ^{Acts 12: 1, 2} His accuser on sighting the extraordinary resilience and faith of James even in the face of death repented and asked James for forgiveness. The apostle kissed him, saying "peace be to thee". He was converted to Christ and was beheaded with James.

JUDAS THADDAEUS

Also called Jude Lebbaeus. He was the brother of James and the son of Alphaeus. He preached the gospel in Persia and Mesopotamia (parts of Iraq and Syria). He was crucified and beaten to death by pagan priests in AD 72. He wrote the epistle of Jude.

MATTHEW

He was the son of Alphaeus (not the same father as James, Judas and Simon *Zelotes*). He was a tax collector (publican) and was called Levi before his call to the ministry by Jesus. He left all he had and followed Jesus. He preached the gospel for 15 years in Judea and then moved out to Egypt and Ethiopia where he also preached the gospel. In AD 60, in the city of Nadabah in Ethiopia, he was axed to death with a halberd. He wrote the gospel of Matthew around AD 50 during his missionary work in Judea.

SIMON ZELOTES

Before his call, he was a *Zelotes* (a fanatic and member of a Jewish rebel group that opposed the Roman rule of Palestine and attempted military overthrows against the Roman rule. They were similar to a political extremist group of today). He became the bishop of the church in Jerusalem at the death of James "the just one". He preached the gospel in Egypt, Mauritania, Libya, other parts of Africa and Britain. He was martyred by Emperor Trajan of Rome in AD 107 because he was feared that as a descendant of David, Simon could claim the throne from him. He was 120 years of age.

PHILIP THE APOSTLE

He was a brother of Bartholomew. He preached the gospel in France, Asia Minor and Southern Russia. He was tortured and crucified in Hierapolis, a city in Phrygia (in present day Turkey) around AD 54.

MATTHIAS

He was the disciple chosen to replace Judas Iscariot when he committed suicide. Matthias was stoned to death and then beheaded by the Jews in Jerusalem.

BARNABAS

He was a companion of the Apostle Paul in the first missionary journey before they parted ways on account of a sharp disagreement they had on whether John Mark, his nephew, should accompany them on their second missionary journey. Acts 15: 37- 39 He preached mainly in Cyprus, his hometown, and was stoned to death by Jews in the region of Salamis in Greece.

JOHN MARK

He accompanied Barnabas and Paul in their first missionary journey but later parted ways with them. He preached the gospel in Egypt and was the first bishop of the church he established in Alexandria. He was killed in Alexandria, AD 68. The account of his death is as follows. As he preached the gospel in the city on a Sunday, the pagans in that city seized him, tied his feet with cords and dragged him along the rocky streets, even as pieces of his flesh tore off and littered the ground. This happened through out the whole day and while it did, he never ceased praising God and thanking Him. At night he was thrown in prison where he was given glorious visions by the Lord Jesus. The next day, he was dragged again in the streets and this continued until he died. He was buried in Alexandria. This disciple, who turned his back on the gospel when he left the missionary company of both Paul and Barnabas, and who also had out of fear for his own life (and made numb to shame) fled naked when Jesus was seized in the Garden of Gethsemane, even though not converted to Jesus at this time, later with inexpressible joy and immense gratitude gave his life for the sake of the gospel of his master Jesus. He felt honoured to be counted worthy to die for Jesus. He was an associate of Apostle Peter, who led him to salvation in Jesus Christ, and he wrote the gospel according to Mark based on the teachings of Peter.

THOMAS

He was also called *Didymus* (the Greek equivalent for "Thomas") and was one of the original twelve apostles of Jesus. His name in both its Hebrew (Thomas) and Greek (Didymus) mean "twin" thus lending the suggestion that he was a twin. He preached the gospel to the Parthians (South West Asia), Medes, Persians, and the Indians where he led many to Christ Jesus. In India, he was seized and tortured with red hot plates by pagan priests and was then cast into a heating furnace which miraculously did not hurt him in anyway. Seeing this, he was then pierced with spears while still in the furnace until he died. His body which was in no way consumed by the furnace was buried in the town of Calamina, India. He died around AD 70.

SIMON PETER

He was the very impulsive disciple that denied the Lord Jesus three times. He along with James and John, formed part of the inner circle of the disciples of Jesus. He preached the gospel in the regions of Babylon (which was his headquarters) (Iraq), [1 Pet. 5: 13] Bithynia and Cappadocia (Turkey), Pontus (North East Asia), and Galatia (Asia Minor). Under Emperor Nero, the persecution of Christians intensified. Peter was seized and cast into a horrible prison called the Mamertine. For months he was manacled to a post and was brutally tortured in this place of hideous darkness. Despite this he preached the gospel to his jailers and led them to salvation in Christ Jesus. While in this place, he also witnessed his wife being led out to be executed, and comfortingly exhorted her to remember the Lord, and not renounce her faith in Him which was a condition for freedom. She kept the faith and was executed. About AD 68, at the orders of Nero, he was crucified head down. He requested to be crucified this way because he did not consider himself worthy to die in the same manner as the Lord Jesus. His manner of death fulfilled what Jesus had told him as recorded in John 21: 18, 19. He this time did not deny his master, but gladly laid down his life for the gospel. He wrote the first and second epistles of Peter.

JOHN

He was called the "beloved disciple" and was regarded as the closest disciple to the Lord Jesus. He was a son of Zebedee and brother of James "the greater". He preached the gospel in Palestine and cities of Western Asia, notably Ephesus where he settled before his death. Emperor Domitian of Rome at this time had begun a fierce and widespread persecution of Christians in the whole Roman Empire. John was captured, brought Rome and immersed in boiling oil. Miraculously, this had no effect on him and so he was exiled to the island of Patmos by the emperor about AD 95. He received visions while on this island which he recorded in the book of Revelation. After the death of Domitian, he was recalled from the island, and he returned to the city of Ephesus. He died naturally about 98 AD at the age of about 100 years. He wrote the gospel according to John, the first, second and third epistles of John, and the book of Revelation.

In his lifetime, he always emphasized on love for the Lord and for the brethren, as is also evidenced in his books. In one instance, when John, being too feeble by reason of advanced age to walk to the Christian assemblies, was carried there by young men, his only address was always: "little children, love one another." When asked why he kept repeating the same words he replied, "Because this is the Lord's command, and enough is done when this is done." In another instance, John entrusted a decent looking youth in the hands of the Bishop at Ephesus. The bishop taught and subsequently baptized the youth but did not establish him in Christ. Returning after a while John said to the bishop: "restore the pledge which I and the Saviour entrusted to you before the congregation." The bishop with tears replied: "he is dead ... dead to God ... a robber!" John replied, "to what a keeper I have entrusted my brother's soul!" John hastened to the robber's fortress. The sentinels brought him before their captain. The captain attempted to flee from him but John said: "why do you flee from me, your father, an unarmed old man? You have yet a hope of life. I will yet give an account to Christ of you. If need be, I will gladly die for you." John never left him until he had rescued him from sin and restored him to Christ.

TIMOTHY

He was a companion of the Apostle Paul, and his "true child in the faith". [1 Tim. 1: 2] He was ordained bishop of the church at Ephesus by Paul about 65 AD and he served in this position for about 15 years. On a certain day in about AD 80, he witnessed a pagan procession of idols, rituals and songs and attempted to stop them by preaching the gospel. The aggravated pagans beat him up, dragged him through the streets, and stoned him to death.

PAUL

This apostle had devoted much of his early years to the persecution of Christians and stopping the spread of the gospel of salvation, but after his miraculous encounter with the Lord Jesus he was never to remain the same for the rest of his life. He afterward traveled far and wide declaring the salvation and wonderful love of Jesus to peoples and nations. For this reason he was arrested by his own people and sent to Rome to be tried by the Roman Emperor Nero, the vilest of all his predecessors and a man who had proclaimed himself the archenemy of God. The trial was a foregone conclusion- he was sentenced to death for the sake of Jesus. Bound by Roman soldiers, he was placed upon a horse and was led out of the city to be executed. At a remote area, he was dismounted from the horse. He was now very old, being physically worn out but not rusted out for the sake of the gospel. A block was placed on the ground and his neck was laid across the block. He probably looked into the skies for the last time in his life and thanked Jesus for the wonderful privilege of serving Him. He knew whom he had believed. The axe head of the executioner gleamed brilliantly in the sunlight as he raised it up. In a moment, it landed heavily on the block with a thud. The head of the Apostle Paul rolled on to the ground. He had fought a good fight, he had finished his course on earth, and he had kept the faith entrusted to him. He had given his very best to Jesus, and the Lord was certainly proud of him.

The Apostle Paul wrote majority of the New Testament books which include the epistles to the Romans, the Corinthians (first and second), the Galatians, the Ephesians, the Philippians, the Colossians, the Thessalonians (first and second), to Timothy (first and second), Titus, and Philemon. He is also believed to have written the epistle to the Hebrews.

Chapter 18

The Bible in a Year

BIBLE STUDY PLAN

"Study to present yourself approved unto God, a workman that needs not to be ashamed, correctly diving the word of truth"

- 2 Timothy 2: 15

$\mathcal{N}$otice that I used the words "bible study" and not "bible reading" or "bible quoting". Study has some depth associated with it which cannot be said of either reading or quoting. Study goes with understanding but you can read or quote scripture without understanding it. Remember, you can only profit from scripture when you understand it, and this comes from studying it. Why? This is because you can do what scripture says and in the right way only when you understand it. God never said we would profit from scripture because we read it or quote from it. No. He said we should study the scripture SO THAT you will live by it (do what it says) and by this, you will be successful. Josh. 1: 8; 1 Tim. 4: 15 Scripture says we should not only be hearers of the word but also doers of it. Jam. 1: 22 The key to acting out the word of God rightly is to understand it rightly and this only comes by spending ample time studying it. The more you study it the more the Holy Spirit reveals Jesus to you. The more you know Jesus the deeper will be your relationship with Him. Scriptures instructs us to KEEP GROWING to the full knowledge of God:

*"...that you might walk worthy of the Lord unto all pleasing, being fruitful in every good work, and INCREASING (Grk. "**auzano**" meaning to "GROW" or "ENLARGE") to the FULL knowledge of God..."* Col. 1: 10

The end result of this is that you will not fall away as a believer. To summarize, the **profit** is in the **doing** and the doing is in the **understanding** and the understanding is in the **studying**.

Do not bother about how to understand scriptures. No man can live the Christian life, let alone understand scriptures on his own. The author of the book is the Holy Spirit; the book is spiritually and not intellectually understood, and it is only the Holy Spirit that can give any man sound understanding of it. The book contains the mind and thoughts of the eternal God which has been put down into concrete readable form in a similar way that a man puts down his ideas into a book or novel for people to read. No one knows the things of a man except the spirit of the man. 1 Cor. 2: 11, 16 Similarly, no one can understand the mind of God except the Spirit of God who now lives in you as a believer. The question is not if the Holy Spirit will help you. He is more than willing to help you than you are ready for it. It is rather a question of if you are willing to spend time under His tutelage. Many are absorbed so deeply into the affairs of this world that they hardly spend time with Him. Remember I described it as enrolling at the University of the Holy Spirit where you should be faithful in attending His lectures. God will not do the aspect of bible study for you, just as your parents would not go to school and study on your behalf, or did not do so. It is your responsibility. God WILL NOT do for you what you should do for yourself. And even more, bible study is **compulsory** for spiritual growth. Read what 1 Peter 2: 2 says:

*"as recently born babies, earnestly desire the pure (sincere; unadulterated) milk of the word, so that you may BE GROWING (Grk. " **auzano**") thereby."*

It is the food of the spirit, and so neglecting it is detrimental to your spirit just as neglecting physical food for too long will in the end be detrimental to your body.

Having noted these, let us now consider how to study the bible.

1. The first thing you must do is to discipline yourself. No man can go far with God without self discipline. Bible study goes with denials- of the flesh and the world, and positions you in a strategic way to constantly communicate with God. Without bible study, you cannot pray. Read what our Lord Jesus says:

    "If you abide in Me, and My words abide in you, you shall ask what you will and it shall be done unto you" Jhn. 15:7

Consider how the original Greek translation puts it:

"If ever you KEEP REMAINING in Me and My words KEEP REMAINING in you, whatever you WANT, request (pray), and it will occur for you"

Now note the continuous tenses used, and the conditions to fulfill before making request for what you want- you keep remaining in Him, and His words keep remaining in you. You need discipline to STUDY this word every day irrespective of how busy you may be.

Another aspect to discipline in bible study is that of timing. There are two facets to this. First, the time you set aside daily for bible study. Second, the length of time set aside for bible study daily. Concerning the first part, so many see bible study as something they just have to do everyday, just as they see prayer. As much as this is good, this by itself is just too shallow and it may end up becoming a burden to such a person. It only points to "religiosity". More importantly, what should drive you to study the bible should not only be because it is necessary or religiously expected of you, but also because of deep thirst for God. If you study scriptures or pray out of deep thirst for God, you will never be burdened by such activities. Such thirst to know more of God will SPONTANEOUSLY drive you in this direction. You will derive great joy from it, and God will reward you. For the second part, the length of time spent in bible study should not be limited by other activities. Never rush in the presence of God. Bible study goes beyond just opening the bible to study. It is the time the Holy Spirit teaches you and reveals the deep things of God to you. In other words, superficially it means opening the bible to study; in actual fact and in a deeper sense, it means spending time with the Holy Spirit. You are sitting in His lecture classroom and He stays beside you as your professor, teaching you all that is necessary for you. As such, when you see it from this angle you then know that He is the one that runs the show and determines how much time you ought to spend with Him in order to learn a certain thing.

2. Get a writing pen and material. I write this to you with every certainty- there will be no occasion you genuinely spend time

with God in bible study that He will not reveal a thing to you or give you a word. Never. During my personal bible study, there are times it comes in torrentially that the only way I can remember all of them is to write them down as quickly as I can and as they come. And as I write them down, He opens up my mind of understanding and reveals even more. The words or revelations that God gives you are too precious to be lost. Losing just one word out of a thousand words spoken by God can be as good as losing every thing. Every word matters; every detail is important. Its sequence and manner of presentation are imperative. The summary of all this is here stated- before undertaking bible study, always have a writing material by your side because you will surely need them.

3. Have a bible concordance. Scripture was not originally written by its inspired writers in English or Spanish or Korean or even the Modern Greek language. It was originally written in Hebrew, Aramaic, and old Greek. Bible study with a concordance not only gives you the original Hebrew or Greek translations, but also gives you cross-references of various verses in scripture. You need not be a bible scholar or Jewish Rabbi or pastor to undertake a study of the bible in the original Hebrew or Greek. Studying this way, you get to know the original thoughts of the authors which they intended to pass across to the readers, but which are not clearly translated or reflected in the English versions. Let us consider one of several instances in the book of Revelation:

> *"And round about the throne were twenty four seats, and upon the seats I saw twenty four elders sitting, clothed in white garments; and they had on their heads CROWNS (Grk. "**stephanos**") of gold"* Rev. 4: 4

> *"And I stood upon the sand of the sea. And I saw a beast rise up out of the sea, having seven heads and ten horns, and upon his horns ten CROWNS (Grk. "**diadema**"), and upon his heads the name of blasphemy"* Rev. 13: 1

Notice that both verses have the same English word "CROWNS", but studying it in the original Greek text in which it was written, the writer, the Apostle John uses two different Greek words for them- ***stephanos*** and ***diadema***. The

Greek word "***stephanos***" means a victor's crown or wreath. This was a crown given to someone who had taken part in a competition or battle and emerged victorious. It is similar to a gold medal presented to a winner in a sport's competition. On the other hand, the Greek word "***diadema***" signifies royalty, or more figuratively, power and authority. It is the Greek word used for the crown of kings and princes.

Therefore, anyone reading these verses in the English version might be led to think that the word CROWNS used in the two verses refer to one and the same thing. But looking this up in a concordance, we find that the Apostle John was referring to two totally different things even though the English version uses the same word. This in turn influences how you understand and further apply those verses practically. The same can be seen in numerous other verses in scripture.

4. Study the bible in a quiet place. Most of the revelations and visions I have received from God came while studying in very tranquil environments. This reduces distractions and helps in fine- tuning your spirit man to listen and receive from God.

5. Study the word prayerfully and expectantly. Ask the Holy Spirit to help you and grant you wisdom and understanding of scriptures. Scriptures instructs us that

> "If anyone of you lack wisdom, let him ask (**Grk. "request"**) of God who gives to all generously and does not reproach, and it shall be given to him" Jam. 1: 5

So many refrain from asking God impressive things and think it is humility. They say things like "whatever God gives me, I will take" or "who am I to request such a thing of the Most High? An ant like me?" Truly, such persons cannot receive from God. Learn this lesson from King Ahaz of Israel. An evil conspiracy had been made against the Southern kingdom of Israel by the kings of two nations- Rezin, the king of Syria, and Remaliah, the king of the Northern kingdom of Israel, to overthrow it and set Rezin king there (ref. Isai. 7: 1-13). The Lord God gave a comforting word to Ahaz through the Prophet Isaiah that such evil conspiracy would never stand or come to pass. Ahaz was further requested to ask God for a sign, no matter how big it was:

"Ask for yourself a sign from the Lord, your God; ask it either IN THE DEPTH or IN THE HEIGHT ABOVE" [v. 11]

God threw this open check to Ahaz, just as He does to His children every day, and here is how Ahaz replied,

"I will not ask, neither will I test the Lord" [v. 12]

Ahaz thought he was displaying great humility, and he expected a wonderful commendation from God for such display. But here is God's reaction to his reply through the Prophet Isaiah,

"Hear you now, O house of David! Is it a little thing for you to weary mortals that you also weary the Lord my God?" [v. 13]

That is the very same attitude of many Christians today. Scriptures is clear about asking God,

*"Ask and you shall receive (**Grk. "request and you shall obtain"**) that your joy may be full (complete)"* [Jhn. 16: 24]

"...let your requests be made known unto God" [Php. 4: 6]

"If you shall ask anything in my name, I will do it" [Jhn. 14: 14]

So it is your duty to ask God, and He expects you to ask Him. God is looking for "ambitious" believers who are prepared to believe and ask Him for the seemingly impossible; and not just minor stuff. Such "ambitious" believers thrill him.

More so, study the word expectantly, and not lackadaisically. Expect to receive a word (*rhema*) from God.

6. Study the New Testament daily. Do not discard the Old Testament but make the New Testament a part of your daily bible study, especially the Acts of the Apostles and the letters (Romans to Jude). These letters were written to the church (believers), instructing and directing them on how they should conduct themselves as Christians. They, in the same way, instruct you on how to live as a Christian. (This is why I have included one New Testament chapter each day in the bible study plan).

7. Outline important points which the Holy Spirit points out to you as you study scripture and memorize each verse. God will surely direct you as you devote yourself to intense bible study, and so you have to be prepared to take notes from Him as He opens up scripture to you.

8. Meditate on the word. To meditate goes beyond just "thinking" on the word of God. The Hebrew translation for "meditate" as found for instance in Joshua 1: 8 is "*hagar*". It means to "**murmur**". Thinking is ONLY AN ASPECT of meditation, but is scripturally NOT MEDITATION as so many assume. Thinking has to do with the mind; murmuring goes beyond the mind to involve the mouth. Murmuring was and is still the Jewish way of meditating on the laws of Moses.

Now here is the bible study guide for you in a year. Be sure to diligently and faithfully study the scriptures.

JANUARY	MORNING	MORNING	EVENING
1	**Genesis** 1- 2	**Matthew** 1	**Esther** 1
2	" 3- 4	" 2	" 2
3	" 5- 6	" 3	" 3
4	" 7- 8	" 4	" 4
5	" 9- 10	" 5	" 5
6	" 11- 12	" 6	" 6
7	" 13- 14	" 7	" 7
8	" 15- 16	" 8	" 8
9	" 17- 18	" 9	" 9
10	"19- 20	" 10	" 10
11	" 21- 22	" 11	**Job** 1
12	" 23- 24	" 12	" 2
13	" 25- 26	" 13	" 3
14	" 27- 28	" 14	" 4
15	" 29- 30	" 15	" 5
16	" 31- 32	" 16	" 6
17	" 33- 34	" 17	" 7
18	" 35- 36	" 18	" 8

JANUARY	MORNING	MORNING	EVENING
19	" 37- 38	" 19	" 9
20	" 39- 40	" 20	" 10
21	" 41- 42	" 21	" 11
22	" 43- 44	" 22	" 12
23	" 45- 46	" 23	" 13
24	" 47- 48	" 24	" 14
25	" 49- 50	" 25	" 15
26	**Exodus** 1- 2	" 26	" 16
27	" 3- 4	" 27	" 17
28	" 5- 6	" 28	" 18
29	" 7- 8	**Mark** 1	" 19
30	" 9- 10	" 2	" 20
31	" 11- 12	" 3	" 21

FEBRUARY	MORNING	MORNING	EVENING
1	**Exodus** 13- 14	**Mark** 4	**Job** 22
2	" 15- 16	" 5	" 23
3	" 17- 18	" 6	" 24
4	" 19- 20	" 7	" 25
5	" 21- 22	" 8	" 26
6	" 23- 24	" 9	" 27
7	" 25- 26	" 10	" 28
8	" 27- 28	" 11	" 29
9	" 29- 30	" 12	" 30
10	" 31- 32	" 13	" 31
11	" 33- 34	" 14	" 32
12	" 35- 36	" 15	" 33
13	" 37- 38	" 16	" 34
14	" 39- 40	**Luke** 1	" 35
15	**Leviticus** 1	" 2	" 36
16	" 2	" 3	" 37
17	" 3	" 4	" 38
18	" 4	" 5	" 39
19	" 5	" 6	" 40
20	" 6	" 7	" 41
21	" 7	" 8	" 42

FEBRUARY	MORNING	MORNING	EVENING
22	" 8	" 9	**Psalms** 1- 3
23	" 9	" 10	" 4- 6
24	" 10	" 11	" 7- 9
25	" 11	" 12	" 10-12
26	" 12	" 13	" 13- 15
27	" 13	" 14	" 16- 18
28	" 14	" 15	" 19- 21
29	" 15	" 16	" 22- 24

MARCH	MORNING	MORNING	EVENING
1	**Leviticus** 16	**Luke** 17	**Psalms** 25- 27
2	" 17	" 18	" 28- 30
3	" 18	" 19	" 31- 33
4	" 19	" 20	" 34- 36
5	" 20	" 21	" 37- 39
6	" 21	" 22	" 40- 42
7	" 22	" 23	" 43- 45
8	" 23	" 24	" 46- 48
9	" 24	**John** 1	" 49- 51
10	" 25	" 2	" 52- 54
11	" 26	" 3	" 55- 57
12	" 27	" 4	" 58- 60
13	**Numbers** 1- 2	" 5	" 61- 63
14	" 3- 4	" 6	" 64- 66
15	" 5- 6	" 7	" 67- 69
16	" 7- 8	" 8	" 70- 72
17	" 9- 10	" 9	" 73- 75
18	" 11- 12	" 10	" 76- 78
19	" 13- 14	" 11	" 79- 81
20	" 15- 16	" 12	" 82- 84
21	" 17- 18	" 13	" 85- 87
22	" 19- 20	" 14	" 88- 90
23	" 21- 22	" 15	" 91- 93
24	" 23- 24	" 16	" 94- 96
25	" 25- 26	" 17	" 97- 99

MARCH	MORNING	MORNING	EVENING
26	" 27- 28	" 18	" 100- 102
27	" 29- 30	" 19	" 103- 105
28	" 31- 32	" 20	" 106- 108
29	" 33- 34	" 21	" 109- 111
30	" 35- 36	**Acts** 1	" 112- 114
31	**Deuteronomy** 1	" 2	" 115- 117

APRIL	MORNING	MORNING	EVENING
1	**Deuteronomy** 2	**Acts** 3	**Psalms** 118- 120
2	" 3	" 4	" 121- 123
3	" 4	" 5	" 124- 126
4	" 5	" 6	" 127- 129
5	" 6	" 7	" 130-132
6	" 7	" 8	" 133-135
7	" 8	" 9	" 136- 138
8	" 9	" 10	" 139- 141
9	" 10	" 11	" 142- 144
10	" 11	" 12	" 145- 147
11	" 12	" 13	" 148- 150
12	" 13	" 14	**Proverbs** 1
13	" 14	" 15	" 2
14	" 15	" 16	" 3
15	" 16	" 17	" 4
16	" 17	" 18	" 5
17	" 18	" 19	" 6
18	" 19	" 20	" 7
19	" 20	" 21	" 8
20	" 21	" 22	" 9
21	" 22	" 23	" 10
22	" 23	" 24	" 11
23	" 24	" 25	" 12
24	" 25	" 26	" 13
25	" 26	" 27	" 14
26	" 27	" 28	" 15
27	" 28	**Romans** 1	" 16
28	" 29	" 2	" 17

APRIL	MORNING	MORNING	EVENING
29	" 30	" 3	" 18
30	" 31	" 4	" 19

MAY	MORNING	MORNING	EVENING
1	**Deuteronomy** 32	**Romans** 5	**Proverbs** 20
2	" 33	" 6	" 21
3	" 34	" 7	" 22
4	**Joshua** 1	" 8	" 23
5	" 2	" 9	" 24
6	" 3	" 10	" 25
7	" 4	" 11	" 26
8	" 5	" 12	" 27
9	" 6	" 13	" 28
10	" 7	" 14	" 29
11	" 8	" 15	" 30
12	" 9	" 16	" 31
13	" 10	**1 Corinthians** 1	**Ecclesiastes** 1
14	" 11	" 2	" 2
15	" 12	" 3	" 3
16	" 13	" 4	" 4
17	" 14	" 5	" 5
18	" 15	" 6	" 6
19	" 16	" 7	" 7
20	" 17	" 8	" 8
21	" 18	" 9	" 9
22	" 19	" 10	" 10
23	" 20	" 11	" 11
24	" 21	" 12	" 12
25	" 22	" 13	**Songs** 1
26	" 23	" 14	" 2
27	" 24	" 15	" 3
28	**Judges** 1	" 16	" 4
29	" 2	**2 Corinthians** 1	" 5
30	" 3	" 2	" 6
31	" 4	" 3	" 7

JUNE	MORNING	MORNING	EVENING
1	**Judges** 5	**2 Corinthians** 4	**Songs** 8
2	" 6	" 5	**Isaiah** 1- 2
3	" 7	" 6	" 3- 4
4	" 8	" 7	" 5- 6
5	" 9	" 8	" 7- 8
6	" 10	" 9	" 9- 10
7	" 11	" 10	" 11- 12
8	" 12	" 11	" 13- 14
9	" 13	" 12	" 15- 16
10	" 14	" 13	" 17-18
11	" 15	**Galatians** 1	" 19- 20
12	" 16	" 2	" 21- 22
13	" 17	" 3	" 23- 24
14	" 18	" 4	" 25- 26
15	" 19	" 5	" 27- 28
16	" 20	" 6	" 29- 30
17	" 21	**Ephesians** 1	" 31- 32
18	**Ruth** 1	" 2	" 33- 34
19	" 2	" 3	" 35- 36
20	" 3	" 4	" 37- 38
21	" 4	" 5	" 39- 40
22	**1 Samuel** 1	" 6	" 41- 42
23	" 2	**Philippians** 1	" 43- 44
24	" 3	" 2	" 45- 46
25	" 4	" 3	" 47- 48
26	" 5	" 4	" 49- 50
27	" 6	**Colossians** 1	" 51- 52
28	" 7	" 2	" 53- 54
29	" 8	" 3	" 55- 56
30	" 9	" 4	" 57- 58

JULY	MORNING	MORNING	EVENING
1	**1 Samuel** 10	**1 Thessalonians** 1	**Isaiah** 59- 60
2	" 11	" 2	" 61- 62
3	" 12	" 3	" 63- 64
4	" 13	" 4	" 65- 66

JULY	MORNING	MORNING	EVENING
5	" 14	" 5	**Jeremiah** 1
6	" 15	**2 Thessalonians** 1	" 2
7	"16	" 2	" 3
8	" 17	" 3	" 4
9	" 18	**1 Timothy** 1	" 5
10	" 19	" 2	" 6
11	" 20	" 3	" 7
12	" 21	" 4	" 8
13	" 22	" 5	" 9
14	" 23	" 6	" 10
15	" 24	**2 Timothy** 1	" 11
16	" 25	" 2	" 12
17	" 26	" 3	" 13
18	" 27	" 4	" 14
19	" 28	**Titus** 1	" 15
20	" 29	" 2	" 16
21	" 30	" 3	" 17
22	" 31	**Philemon** 1	" 18
23	**2 Samuel** 1	**Hebrews** 1	" 19
24	" 2	" 2	" 20
25	" 3	" 3	" 21
26	" 4	" 4	" 22
27	" 5	" 5	" 23
28	" 6	" 6	" 24
29	" 7	" 7	" 25
30	" 8	" 8	" 26
31	" 9	" 9	" 27

AUGUST	MORNING	MORNING	EVENING
1	**2 Samuel** 10	**Hebrews** 10	**Jeremiah** 28
2	" 11	" 11	" 29
3	" 12	" 12	" 30
4	" 13	" 13	" 31
5	" 14	**James** 1	" 32
6	" 15	" 2	" 33
7	" 16	" 3	" 34

AUGUST	MORNING	MORNING	EVENING
8	" 17	" 4	" 35
9	" 18	" 5	" 36
10	" 19	**1 Peter** 1	" 37
11	" 20	" 2	" 38
12	" 21	" 3	" 39
13	" 22	" 4	" 40
14	" 23	" 5	" 41
15	" 24	**2 Peter** 1	" 42
16	**1 Kings** 1	" 2	" 43
17	" 2	" 3	" 44
18	" 3	**1 John** 1	" 45
19	" 4	" 2	" 46
20	" 5	" 3	" 47
21	" 6	" 4	" 48
22	" 7	" 5	" 49
23	" 8	**2 John** 1	" 50
24	" 9	**3 John** 1	" 51
25	" 10	**Jude** 1	" 52
26	" 11	**Revelation** 1	**Lamentations** 1
27	" 12	" 2	" 2
28	" 13	" 3	" 3
29	" 14	" 4	" 4
30	" 15	" 5	" 5
31	" 16	" 6	**Ezekiel** 1

SEPTEMBER	MORNING	MORNING	EVENING
1	**1 Kings** 17	**Revelation** 7	**Ezekiel** 2
2	" 18	" 8	" 3
3	" 19	" 9	" 4
4	" 20	" 10	" 5
5	" 21	" 11	" 6
6	" 22	" 12	" 7
7	**2 Kings** 1	" 13	" 8
8	" 2	" 14	" 9
9	" 3	" 15	" 10
10	" 4	" 16	" 11
11	" 5	" 17	" 12

SEPTEMBER	MORNING	MORNING	EVENING
12	" 6	" 18	" 13
13	" 7	" 19	" 14
14	" 8	" 20	" 15
15	" 9	" 21	" 16
16	" 10	" 22	" 17
17	" 11	**Mark** 1	" 18
18	" 12	" 2	" 19
19	" 13	" 3	" 20
20	" 14	" 4	" 21
21	" 15	" 5	" 22
22	" 16	" 6	" 23
23	" 17	" 7	" 24
24	" 18	" 8	" 25
25	" 19	" 9	" 26
26	" 20	" 10	" 27
27	" 21	" 11	" 28
28	" 22	" 12	" 29
29	" 23	" 13	" 30
30	" 24	" 14	" 31

OCTOBER	MORNING	MORNING	EVENING
1	**2 Kings** 25	**Mark** 15	**Ezekiel** 32
2	**1 Chronicles** 1	" 16	" 33
3	" 2	**Luke** 1	" 34
4	" 3	" 2	" 35
5	" 4	" 3	" 36
6	" 5	" 4	" 37
7	" 6	" 5	" 38
8	" 7	" 6	" 39
9	" 8	" 7	" 40
10	" 9	" 8	" 41
11	" 10	" 9	" 42
12	" 11	" 10	" 43
13	" 12	" 11	" 44
14	" 13	" 12	" 45
15	" 14	" 13	" 46

16	" 15	" 14	" 47
17	" 16	" 15	" 48
18	" 17	" 16	**Daniel** 1
19	" 18	" 17	" 2
20	" 19	" 18	" 3
21	" 20	" 19	" 4
22	" 21	" 20	" 5
23	" 22	" 21	" 6
24	" 23	" 22	" 7
25	" 24	" 23	" 8
26	" 25	" 24	" 9
27	" 26	**Acts** 1	" 10
28	" 27	" 2	" 11
29	" 28	" 3	" 12
30	" 29	" 4	**Hosea** 1
31	**2 Chronicles** 1	" 5	" 2

NOVEMBER	MORNING	MORNING	EVENING
1	**2 Chronicles** 2	**Acts** 6	**Hosea** 3
2	" 3	" 7	" 4
3	" 4	" 8	" 5
4	" 5	" 9	" 6
5	" 6	" 10	" 7
6	" 7	" 11	" 8
7	" 8	" 12	" 9
8	" 9	" 13	" 10
9	" 10	" 14	" 11
10	" 11	" 15	" 12
11	" 12	" 16	" 13
12	" 13	" 17	" 14
13	" 14	" 18	**Amos** 1
14	" 15	" 19	" 2
15	" 16	" 20	" 3
16	" 17	" 21	" 4
17	" 18	" 22	" 5
18	" 19	" 23	" 6
19	" 20	" 24	" 7
20	" 21	" 25	" 8

NOVEMBER	MORNING	MORNING	EVENING
21	" 22	" 26	" 9
22	" 23	" 27	Obadiah 1
23	" 24	" 28	Jonah 1
24	" 25	Romans 1	" 2
25	" 26	" 2	" 3
26	" 27	" 3	" 4
27	" 28	" 4	Micah 1
28	" 29	" 5	" 2
29	" 30	" 6	" 3
30	" 31	" 7	" 4

DECEMBER	MORNING	MORNING	EVENING
1	2 Chronicles 32	Romans 8	Micah 5
2	" 33	" 9	" 6
3	" 34	" 10	" 7
4	" 35	" 11	Nahum 1
5	" 36	" 12	" 2
6	Ezra 1	" 13	" 3
7	" 2	" 14	Habakkuk 1
8	" 3	" 15	" 2
9	" 4	" 16	" 3
10	" 5	Revelation 1	Zephaniah 1
11	" 6	" 2	" 2
12	" 7	" 3	" 3
13	" 8	" 4	Haggiah 1- 2
14	" 9	" 5	Zechariah 1
15	" 10	" 6	" 2
16	Nehemiah 1	" 7	" 3
17	" 2	" 8	" 4
18	" 3	" 9	" 5
19	" 4	" 10	" 6
20	" 5	" 11	" 7
21	" 6	" 12	" 8
22	" 7	" 13	" 9
23	" 8	" 14	" 10
24	" 9	" 15	" 11

DECEMBER	MORNING	MORNING	EVENING
25	" 10	" 16	" 12
26	" 11	" 17	" 13
27	" 12	" 18	" 14
28	" 13	" 19	**Malachi** 1
29	**Joel** 1	" 20	" 2
30	" 2	" 21	" 3
31	" 3	" 22	" 4